Scripture Unbound

Scripture Unbound

A UNITARIAN UNIVERSALIST APPROACH

Jonalu Johnstone

Skinner House Books
BOSTON

www.skinnerhouse.org

Printed in the United States

Cover design by Kathryn Sky-Peck
Text design by Jeff Miller

print ISBN: 978-1-55896-846-2
eBook ISBN: 978-1-55896-847-9

6 5 4 3 2 1
23 22 21 20 19

Names: Johnstone, Jonalu, 1955- author.
Title: Scripture unbound : a Unitarian Universalist approach / Jonalu Johnstone.
Description: Boston : Skinner House Books, 2019. | Includes bibliographical
    references.
Identifiers: LCCN 2019028947 (print) | LCCN 2019028948 (ebook) |
    ISBN 9781558968462 (paperback) | ISBN 9781558968479 (ebook)
Subjects: LCSH: Sacred books. | Unitarian Universalist churches—Doctrines.
Classification: LCC BL71 .J64 2019 (print) | LCC BL71 (ebook) |
    DDC 208/.2—dc23
LC record available at https://lccn.loc.gov/2019028947
LC ebook record available at https://lccn.loc.gov/2019028948

We are grateful for permission to reprint the following: *The Illustrated I Ching*, translated by R. L. Wing, trans. ©1982 by Immedia; used by permission of Doubleday, an imprint of the Knopf Doubleday Publishing Group, a division of Random House LLC; all rights reserved. From *Tao Teh Ching*, by Lao Tzu, Translated by John C. H. Wu, ©1990; reprinted by arrangement with Shambhala Publications, Inc., Boston, MA, www.shambhala.com. The Scripture quotations contained herein are from the *New Revised Standard Version Bible*, copyright © 1989 by the Division of Christian Education of the National Council of the Churches of Christ in the U.S.A., and are used by permission; all rights reserved.

Contents

INTRODUCTION   vii
A Reading from Esther 4:13–5:3   xxi

PART I
Traditional Tools and Readings of Scripture   1

CHAPTER ONE *Scripture and Community*   3
A Reading from the Analects of Confucius 2:2–4   9

CHAPTER TWO *Scripture and Authority*   13
A Reading from Nehemiah 8:1–10   35

CHAPTER THREE *Historical-Critical Reading*   41
A Reading from the Qur'an 3:1–7   55

CHAPTER FOUR *Contextual Criticism*   59
A Reading from Luke 10:38–42   71

CHAPTER FIVE *Scripture in Spiritual Practice*   75
A Reading from Genesis Midrash Rabbah 8:5   97

CHAPTER SIX *The Question of Translation*   103
A Reading of I Ching 17   113

PART II
A Unitarian Universalist Take on Scripture 119

CHAPTER SEVEN *How Unitarian Universalists Perceive Scripture* 121
A Reading of "For So the Children Come" 135

CHAPTER EIGHT *Preconceptions and Cultural Bias* 139
A Reading from Black Elk Speaks 157

PART III
Using Scripture 165

CHAPTER NINE *Study* 167
A Reading from Dhammapada 1:1–2 177

CHAPTER TEN *Scripture in Worship* 183
A Reading from Isaiah 61:1–4 193

CHAPTER ELEVEN *Beyond Study and Worship* 199
A Reading from the Tao Te Ching 17 209

APPENDIX *Suggested Scriptures and Stories for Theme-Based Ministry* 213

Resources 221
Notes 225

Introduction

When I was a child, I spoke like a child, I thought
like a child, I reasoned like a child; when I became
an adult, I put an end to childish ways.

1 Corinthians 13:11, The Bible,
New Revised Standard Version

I LOVE SCRIPTURE. I have loved scripture for as long as I can
remember.

Growing up in Southern Baptist churches, each Saturday
I pored over the magazine-style quarterly that contained our
weekly lessons, preparing for Sunday school. Each lesson
included a Bible passage, usually a story, with descriptions of
its context and location, and how the people of the time lived.
I studied maps and imagined the story happening. I memorized the verse or two suggested. I tried to figure out the impli-
cations of the lesson for my own life. On Sunday mornings,
our teacher would tell the story, and we'd work on some project related to it. Sunday evenings at Baptist Training Union,
we'd compete in sword drills to see who could find Bible verses
most quickly. During junior high, I attained the Queen step in
our Girls Auxiliary group, for which, wearing a long white

gown, I had to recite and interpret a chapter of the book of Esther in front of the gathered congregation; if memory serves, it was chapter 5.

When I was about twelve, I decided to read the Bible cover to cover—and did. Not that I understood it all, but I persisted and met my goal. Around then, I also discovered my first book of biblical interpretation, *The Bible and the Common Reader*, by novelist and English professor Mary Ellen Chase. Though basic in its approach, it helped me gain a wider perspective of what scripture was.

Despite all of this, reading scripture ultimately led me right out of the church. I couldn't find anywhere in the Bible that God determined to condemn good people to hell for eternity. Though I didn't know it at the time, I followed the same path as eighteenth- and nineteenth-century Universalists—directly to heresy. With great relief, in my mid-twenties, I discovered Unitarian Universalism, where I no longer had to worry about God or salvation—or scripture.

But scripture kept its hold on me. Biblical stories and characters gnawed at me. To me, they were as real as any historical figure, whether or not they had ever existed. Queen Esther still inspired me to stand up for what was right, even at personal cost. Jesus' admonition to care for the poor and visit the sick spoke to me. The prophets exhorted me. The Psalms comforted me. Even when I discovered feminist theology and found my way back to a belief in a new kind of God, I never completely rejected the scriptures I grew up with.

At Harvard Divinity School, studying for Unitarian Universalist ministry, I encountered scripture from various religious traditions and learned that not every tradition looks at scripture as Christians do. Even among Christian sects, I found wide disagreement about how to read and interpret the Bible. I discovered that the Hebrew Scriptures (also called the Hebrew Bible) share many of the same books as the Old Testament but have their own order and interpretation. Hindu scripture could fill a library, while the Qur'an isn't considered authoritative unless it's in Arabic. Thinkers like Mircea Eliade and Ninian Smart, who compared concepts and myths across cultures and traditions, breathed life into philosophy and spirituality for me by cultivating story. And Unitarian minister Von Ogden Vogt's work on liturgy expanded my understanding of the use of scripture in worship, as well as my very definition of scripture.

Though the Christian Bible remains central for me, I find inspiration in the Taoist Tao Te Ching and Chuang Tzu, in the Buddhist Dhammapada, and in the Hindu Bhagavad-Gita. I have taught classes in the church on techniques for reading scripture, as well as on the scriptures themselves, the Christian Bible, and a variety of Taoist, Buddhist, Hindu, Jewish, and Muslim texts.

Western scholarship has tended to overlook the possibility that any human expression other than written text can be scriptural. However, I believe that certain art and architecture—even scientific works such as the Mayan calendar—have scriptural overtones. For example, for centuries Christian stories were taught through icons, stained glass, and other artwork. The Ten Ox-Herding Pictures, long contemplated and commented upon by Zen Buddhists, teach lessons and merit study. Many traditions have elaborate oral traditions and stories that either supplement or substitute for the written word.

While the value and sacredness of these other forms must be acknowledged, the written word has held a special power through the ages and across many cultures. Written scripture also tends to generate more resistance and controversy than scripture in other forms. This book concentrates primarily on the written word, as read and interpreted, rather than on other forms of holy work.

What Is Scripture?

Before we go any further, let's clarify what we mean by the word *scripture*. Many would answer the question "What is scripture?" simply by identifying those texts that are officially designated as sacred by their own tradition. If you ask a Methodist Christian and a Catholic Christian, for instance, the answers may sound the same: "The Bible." If you probe a bit more closely, however, the answers are not identical. Catholic scriptures include the Old Testament and New Testament of the Methodists, plus several books in the Apocrypha omitted by Protestant Christians. Ask a Buddhist to define scripture, and the answer will depend on whether they are Mahayana or Theravada.

But those devoted to Confucian and Taoist religions might stare blankly at the question, because the concept of scripture itself is foreign to them. Instead, they focus on texts designated as "classics," recognizing that these texts are human-created and often attributed to one of the founders of their movements. Confucian tradition names Four Books and Five Classics in particular as foundational. Broadly, though, these and several others are considered classics. Some are well-known outside of China, like the Tao Te Ching (Taoist) and the Analects of Confucius (Confucian), while others, like Wen-Tzu (Taoist) and Book of Odes (Confucian), are recognized mostly by scholars.

So, how do we identify a particular text as scriptural? Many use the term *sacred text* as interchangeable with *scripture*, but religious groups define *sacred* in different ways. Some religious traditions teach that God gave particular books to their people, and only those rise to the rank of scripture. Other traditions regard scripture as a human creation that may or may not be inspired by God.

The simplicity of defining scripture as "sacred text" may mislead in other ways as well. A person may think of a text as sacred to them individually. And while I certainly endorse a wide and inclusive view of what can be considered sacred, for the purposes of this book we will focus on the specific role of a text in the context of a religious community and, ultimately, on the potential role of touchstone texts for Unitarian Universalist communities.

To that end, *scripture* in this book will refer to texts that are affirmed by a community for their spiritual authority and that the community finds normative for good living, calls on for ritual, and uses to guide spiritual growth and development. By using this definition of scripture rather than one particular to any single tradition, I will of necessity sometimes use the word to apply to works that are not considered canonical scripture within their own traditions. It's also important to note that under this definition, it's possible for a Unitarian Universalist community to regard a text as scriptural even if it is not regarded as such within its tradition of origin. I will, however, provide context about the scriptural status of each text within its own tradition to avoid inaccurate or misleading impressions of that tradition's teaching and practice.

Why Study Scripture?

Scripture, like religion itself, wields its influence in ever-widening concentric circles, beginning within ourselves. Scripture can lead us as individuals toward transformation. When we hold and read books that have survived for centuries, we take a step on a personal spiritual journey. There is something about reading a text that is revered by a community, with a reach that is often worldwide and handed down through millennia. The practice of applying it to our own lives can help us feel less alone and more connected to a truth larger than ourselves. It prompts us to examine how we are called to be and what we are called to do in this world. This reflection is the beginning of wisdom. Scripture, then, can illuminate how, individually and collectively, we have come to where we are, and can push us toward more profound truth.

In terms of understanding our Unitarian Universalist heritage, early Unitarians and Universalists were biblical people, immersed in the stories and symbols of Jewish and Christian scripture. Many of them reached their so-called heretical positions through Bible study, as we'll see in chapter 7. By the nineteenth century, some of our Unitarian forebears had discovered the scriptures of other religious traditions, bringing these into our culture. Ralph Waldo Emerson first obtained a copy of the Bhagavad-Gita in 1845,[1] and it has been argued that Eastern religious thought seeped into Transcendentalism, which has influenced Unitarian and Unitarian Universalist theology ever since.

We all come from somewhere. None of us live in a cultural void. Whatever our faith background, educational background, reading habits, or media consumption, we have been shaped both subtly and directly by concentric circles of culture: our families, our communities, our faith traditions, and our nations. And all of these cultural circles inevitably have some relationship to scripture. Even antagonism or indifference to scripture has an effect on how we understand ourselves and how we relate to each other. We have conscious knowledge of some of these influences, while others enter our blood without our complete awareness, especially those that come through story and image. They work on us deeply, as dreams do. We live in them and sometimes don't even notice their effect on our points of view or our arguments. If we don't know our cultural history and sources, though, we can't fully know ourselves.

Biblical mythology runs through American culture. There are so many wonderful examples. David stands up to Goliath in 1 Samuel in the Hebrew Bible, and we draw from that story every time a small, more vulnerable individual or group stands up against oppression, bullying, or a better-equipped foe. Jesus had a vision of a "shining city on a hill" in the Sermon on the Mount in the gospel of Matthew, and this vision has echoed down the centuries through the words of John Winthrop and Ronald Reagan. The story of Moses and the Exodus weaves through the African-American struggle for freedom in the nineteenth century and the Civil Rights Movement of the twentieth, arriving at the contemporary Passover Seder.

Today our world grows more connected through global communications and trade, while our communities diversify. The people we meet—even our next-door neighbors—often come from cultures and religious traditions other than our own. If we have some acquaintance with the values and tenets of their scriptures, we have a greater opportunity for empathy and connection with them, as well as a deeper understanding of the huge geopolitical forces at work around the world. We can be more empowered. If we have some familiarity with the Qur'an, for example, we are better equipped to counter the attacks of bigots against Islam. A broader knowledge of world scripture helps us place ourselves in the context of our modern world.

Among the six Sources of our Unitarian Universalist living tradition, we claim Jewish and Christian teachings, as well as wisdom from the world's religions. We have looked to texts from around the world, from varied and diverse cultures. And as individuals, Unitarian Universalists come from a broad range of spiritual and religious backgrounds, each with their own connections to particular scriptural sources. What's more, our intellectual curiosity invites us to learn more about our neighbors.

Though we may not view the New Testament and Hebrew Scriptures as divinely inspired, the Qur'an as dictated by God, or the Vedas as *apaurusheyatva*, we can appreciate the texts as gifts to humanity. We understand that, through the ages, these works have shaped whole societies and civilizations. We can honor and appreciate them as sources of wisdom that speak to us across generations and cultures. This attitude toward scripture places Unitarian Universalism in a position distinct from other faiths; rather than venerate one text over others, we feel free to read each in the light of all the others.

Resistance

At the same time, many contemporary Unitarian Universalists approach the very idea of scripture with a healthy dose of skepticism. Scientific thought influences us deeply. Many of us recognized contradictions in the scriptures we grew up with, which began our journey to Unitarian Universalism. Often, we continue to struggle with scriptures and interpretations forced upon us earlier in life, or literal understandings that fall short of reason. Our approach to scriptures, then, must acknowledge and wrestle with our doubt.

Many contemporary people find ancient writings culturally distant and irrelevant. Indeed, taken out of the context in which it was written, scripture can be hard to make sense of. To some of us, it seems rigid or, worse, a tool with which elite groups have maintained power and order, suppressed those who are different, and forced people to follow narrow paths of behavior.

No one can deny that texts have been misused though the centuries for these purposes. Studying scripture can be challenging in other ways too, as we encounter worldviews distant from our own, assertions that conflict with scientific understanding, and broad cultural differences. Yet, as I read scriptures, I find they address topics I still struggle with: mortality, relationships, ethics, war, and peace. They speculate on where human beings come from, what our tasks on earth might be, and how we can best live with one another. If we Unitarian Universalists truly value the pursuit of truth and meaning, how can we dismiss what has brought meaning to so many generations? Countless people have found inspiration in books set aside as special by their traditions. If so many have found so much wisdom in a text, there must be something there that can speak to us even today. In our rapidly changing world, we must strive to protect the valuable lessons of the past. We may even find inspiration and guidance for our individual lives hidden in those treasured words.

The goal of this book is to question common assumptions about scripture and help readers open up to new ways of thinking about it and engaging with it, remaining committed to the Unitarian Universalist affirmation of the free and responsible quest for meaning. I hope to illustrate that in reading scripture we may discover—rather than rigidity—nuance, depth, and a wealth of material that generates new ideas, impressions, and interpretations.

Interpretations

None of this means that scriptural texts are easy to approach. The first step is to let go of our own preconceptions. Rather than eyeing the text with mistrust, we can engage directly with it with curiosity. What stories or teachings are conveyed? What images does it evoke? How does it remind us of our own experiences?

Another step is to discern what the text has meant over time. This requires going to a deeper level of inquiry by seeking out secondary sources or interpreters who have written and taught about the text, or to notes included in the published versions we have read. How did the book come to be written? Who wrote it, and what were they trying to accomplish by writing it? What did the text mean to the people who first read it? How did it come to be authoritative? What has it meant through the years to people who have treasured it and let it guide their lives?

Contrary to popular perception in modern Western culture, when we widen our view to include a variety of traditions over the course of history, we find that scripture has relatively rarely been understood as literal truth. Most books have been widely interpreted by different branches or sects of a particular tradition and, sometimes, more than one tradition. We can't say that any of these books have a singular, clear meaning. Such a statement limits authentic engagement with a book. The texts survive because people have been able to mine them for powerful lessons, rather than literal instruction.

Even the most freethinking Unitarian Universalist may encounter surprising familiarity and comfort in the ways adherents of various traditions understand and relate to their tradition's scripture. As we search, we'll have to hold lenses of both doubt and trust in our hands. We can be open to multiple understandings, holding each lightly. We can ask, "Could this be what is said?" rather than pushing away a text that at first seems easy to dismiss. And when we hit a resistant place, we can unpack the preconceptions that we bring that might prejudice us against a text. Throughout this journey, we'll explore a uniquely Unitarian Universalist approach to scripture, informed by skepticism as well as by the free and responsible search for truth and meaning.

Structure

This book takes a broad view of scriptures and classics. In Part I of this book, we will see how traditions view their own formative texts. Rather than delve into each particular religion's sources, we will consider the big picture of scripture, tapping into particular traditions to illustrate general approaches and principles. We will examine ways to talk about scriptures across traditions, rather than narrowing in on an individual religion. Such an approach helps acknowledge important commonalities—for example, how Taoism and Confucianism arose side by side, and how Hinduism and Buddhism grew from similar rootstock, as did Judaism, Christianity, and Islam. We strive to capture broad, overlapping swaths, rather than an in-depth analysis of individual traditions.

This is a good place to acknowledge my own cultural location and internalized biases. I claim my identities as white, female, cisgender, and lesbian, all of which shape my perceptions As someone who is less a scholar than a curious observer, I am most familiar with Western, particularly Christian, understandings of how to engage with ancient religious traditions. Though I am acquainted with other texts and religious ideas, I have never been as immersed in them as I have been in the Christian Bible.

Unitarian Universalism itself emerged out of Christianity. It resonates most deeply—and argues most passionately—

with Christianity. Within the UU cultural context, we are at once most familiar with *and* most frustrated with Christian understandings.

As Unitarian Universalists, though, we have long been conversant with other traditions, and are learning to stretch beyond our particular identities. We wouldn't be true to our own religious understandings of the world if we were to ignore an opportunity to learn from traditions that are less familiar. Perfect understanding is unrealistic, of course, but we can move toward a more complex and nuanced grasp of the gifts these traditions have left us. I'm grateful for the several reviewers who have offered their wisdom, pointed out inaccuracies, and greatly improved what this book has to offer.

Part II examines an explicitly Unitarian Universalist understanding of scripture, one that embraces UU openness to a variety of sources, both traditional and unorthodox. Having learned in Part I about how various cultures and communities define and relate to formative texts, readers should now feel empowered to consider a uniquely Unitarian Universalist approach to the identification, study, and use of keystone texts that we claim as scriptural. We will consider how to define scripture inclusively across traditions and how we might use scriptures from other traditions while steering clear of cultural appropriation. Can we define particular scriptures as our own? Is it possible to introduce texts not called scripture by any other religious group?

Finally, Part III invites us into application. Traditional Christian churches expect an understanding of the Bible to influence every aspect of their congregational culture. One reason Christians study the Bible is to help them shape their

Christian communities. As Unitarian Universalists, we might also find ways to use scripture, both in our congregations and as individuals, to enrich, energize, and revitalize our lives. Our tradition does not restrict these practices to ministers, so lay leaders, too, can seek out opportunities to apply scripture to worship, education, and congregational life, working with their minister in churches where there is one, or as leaders of lay-led societies. Such application may mix traditional understandings with Unitarian Universalist approaches.

Following each chapter, you'll find a short passage from a spiritual source, along with an interpretation I have developed. In each case, the interpretation strives to illustrate some aspect of the approach taken in the chapter. Passages are not selected for their prominence in their original tradition, nor to suggest a special importance of their message. Rather, they are meant to illustrate the principle and give the reader an idea of how to interact with texts themselves. Your personal motivations for engaging with scripture will shape which methods resonate most with you. I hope you will find something that engages your imagination and broadens your understanding.

I invite you on a journey of reading and digesting scripture. I hope the trek leads you to develop inspiration and wisdom. Maybe it will even help you take a step along your own spiritual path.

But first, take a look at this chapter's scripture reading, which contains the passage that was so meaningful to me when I was young.

A Reading from Esther

Mordecai [sent Esther a message:]: "Do not think that
in the king's palace you will escape any more than all
the other Jews. . . . Who knows? Perhaps you have
come to royal dignity for just such a time as this."
Then Esther said in reply to Mordecai, "Go, gather
all the Jews to be found in Susa, and hold a fast on
my behalf, and neither eat nor drink for three days,
night or day. I and my maids will also fast as you do.
After that I will go to the king, though it is against
the law; and if I perish, I perish." Mordecai then went
away and did everything as Esther had ordered him.

On the third day Esther put on her royal robes and
stood in the inner court of the king's palace, opposite
the king's hall. The king was sitting on his royal
throne inside the palace opposite the entrance to
the palace. As soon as the king saw Queen Esther
standing in the court, she won his favor and he held
out to her the golden scepter that was in his hand.
Then Esther approached and touched the top of
the scepter. The king said to her, "What is it, Queen
Esther? What is your request? It shall be given you,
even to the half of my kingdom."

> Esther 4:13–5:3, The Bible,
> New Revised Standard Version

We enter this story at a climactic moment. Esther's cousin Mordecai, who has raised her from childhood, urges her to action: "Who knows? Perhaps you have come to royal dignity for just such a time as this." The words "for . . . such a time as this" echo forcefully. The phrase has become a contemporary Christian ballad and is used across the theological spectrum among Christians as a call to ministry. Esther, as queen, is the only Jew positioned to act.

No one is allowed to enter the king's hall unless they have been sent for. The penalty for unauthorized entry is death. One might think a queen would be exempt. But in the first chapter of the book of Esther, King Ahasuerus banished Queen Vashti, whom Esther has replaced. Queens had no protection from the absolute ruler, so Esther takes a great risk to approach the king.

What could make her do such a thing? Her people, the Jews, are in peril. She wants to save them, as their annihilation has been ordered by the king. Mordecai pushes her, the Jewish people support her, but Esther alone has to take the risk. She has hidden her Jewish heritage, so the king does not know. To save her people, she must risk her life again by confessing her ethnicity. She has prepared for the moment with fasting, and her community has supported her with it.

Reading this text as a pre-teen moved me. I knew little about how to read scripture, except to sink into the story. I did know the feeling of fear that I imagined Esther must have felt. I knew fear of the dark, fear of heights, fear of dogs, fear of disappointing those I loved—and had already worked strenuously to overcome such fears. I had learned to recognize injustice. I had seen homeless people sleeping on the streets of Washington, D.C., encountered bullying in school, and witnessed racial inequality. I realized that I needed courage to counter fears about confronting injustice, just as I had conquered climbing trees and petting dogs, but I wasn't quite sure how to muster it.

Esther gave me an example. She faced a powerful man who had the power of life and death. She broke a rule to come into the court. And she won. There is more plot to unfold in the story, but once Ahasuerus extends the scepter and accepts her presence—and offers her as much as half his kingdom!—her cause is won.

For me, that moment, the pause before entering the court, became a touchstone through my early decades. When I had to enter the principal's office to answer for the politically charged message in the introduction to the yearbook I edited; when I addressed a legislative committee investigating conditions at the residential school where I worked; when I sat in the courtroom in support of a teacher fired for her sexual orientation, despite connections between the school and the organization I worked for; when I spoke out, as I learned to over the years, for the dispossessed and for myself; in all these times, I called on the image and courage of Esther. My fast was stepping into her shoes to equip myself to make that walk into the court. I lived into the story to awaken my own courage, to set aside my own fears. If Esther could do it, so could I!

Years later I learned that the book of Esther was controversial. Martin Luther thought it should be excluded from the Bible because it made no mention of God. I had never noticed the lack of that word because it was clear to me that faithfulness pervaded the book—faithfulness, loyalty, and determination to stand against injustice. Esther was no perfect Jew; she had to step away from her people to marry a foreign ruler.

Hiding her Jewishness must have meant letting go of many ritual practices. Yet, she remained loyal to her people and steadfast in her identity. Mordecai represents the more traditional Jew. Esther connects with Mordecai and with the Jewish community only through messages, but she is never completely apart from community. She invites the people into her experience and even has her maids fast with her. As different as Mordecai and Esther are in their practice of faith, they both demonstrate faithful approaches to living, and they both have the courage to step forward, seemingly alone, but always with others supporting them.

Immersing oneself in the story is one way of reading and interpreting scripture, and it is in some ways the most basic, easily accessible way. Yet, it requires us to suspend our disbelief, which is sometimes challenging. To fully engage with a story, however, we don't have to believe it to be literally true. While Esther is more likely an historical novella than actual history, her story forms the basis of the raucous Jewish holiday of Purim.

Throughout this book, we will review many different ways of reading scripture. We will explore the ways in which cultural, historical, and political context can shed light on the ancient written word, and how contemporary issues can shape our reactions. It is incredibly valuable to know how to explore scripture in many dimensions, but I start here with my personal relationship to this story to make a point I hope you will keep in mind as you move through the book: With or without formal, structured training, everyone can identify with characters, follow a plot, and find lessons in a well-told tale. Though I've since learned scholarly ways of thinking about texts, listening to the story will always hold meaning for me.

PART I

*Traditional Tools
and Readings of
Scripture*

CHAPTER ONE

Scripture and Community

Good Knowing Advisors, all Sutras and writings of
the Great and Small Vehicles, the twelve divisions
of Sutras, have been devised because of people and
established because of the nature of wisdom. If
there were no people the ten thousand dharmas
would not exist. Therefore you should know that
all dharmas are originally postulated because of
people, and all Sutras are spoken for their sakes.

> The Platform Sutra Chapter 2 (Ch'an Buddhism),
> Buddhist Text Translation Society

PEOPLE IN various cultures throughout written history have
designated certain stories, laws, and words of wisdom as special, set-apart, or holy. Some have asserted that God gave
these books to their particular ethnic group, or to the world.
The people may have honored the words through repetition
and taught them to their children. Nineteenth-century jour-
nalist and satirist Ambrose Bierce, in *The Devil's Dictionary*,
defined scriptures as the "sacred books of our holy religion, as
distinguished from the false and profane writings on which all
other faiths are based."

Bierce mocks the intolerance and closed-mindedness that can distinguish sectarian thought, and the history of religion demonstrates the kind of dichotomy he suggests. Indeed, sometimes the religions that are closest, that even share particular scriptures, can be the most at odds about what counts as scripture.

What makes a book scripture within its tradition? Religion scholars Ninian Smart and Richard Hecht struggled with this question as they created an anthology.[2] Traditionally, the definition is through a canon, a definitive list of what books or stories are in, and what are out. This is one of the preconceptions about scripture that generates resistance in a lot of Unitarian Universalists, who don't like to have religious authority imposed upon them even by their own religious leaders. But the truth is that not every religious group has a defined, authoritative set of texts. Buddhists tend to have collections rather than canons. Within a particular religious tradition, not everyone agrees with what's in and what's out. Particular groups—like Mormons and Christian Scientists—add new scriptures to more widely accepted canons. Even Hecht and Smart, who emphasize the importance of canon as defining and giving authority to a text, do not limit themselves as they come to understand the relationship of various religious communities to canonical texts. Instead, they add in many other books that no one has stamped with any official approval. Indeed, they go well beyond even religious texts to identify those sacred to secular groups and ideologies. As they say, "Mao has a place beside the Tao,"[3] meaning that because a group of people—late twentieth-century Chinese Communists—treated *Chairman Mao's Little Red Book* as a text to guide their society, it earns a special status shared by older writings, like the Tao Te Ching, that are recognized as special.

Wilfred Cantwell Smith, the twentieth-century professor of comparative religion, may help us acknowledge the tenuous lines between scripture and non-scripture. In his book *What Is Scripture? A Comparative Approach*, Smith describes scripture not as a book but as a "human activity."[4] In the West, the word *scripture* originally applied only to the "word of God," which Christians took to be what they called the Old Testament and New Testament. Gradually, the concept opened to include holy books from other traditions. Western Christians saw the similarity between how other people treated their books and how they saw their own Bible. In many religious traditions, scripture has value as a symbol of faith as well as a value based on its contents, so adherents treat the physical book itself with reverence by putting it in a special place, kissing it, or including it in ritual. The key to understanding what scripture is lies in recognizing that it is a relational term. In other words, it's about a particular people and their view of the book, not about the book itself. Scripture lives and interacts with a group of people, influencing them and being influenced by them. What is in the texts does not matter nearly as much as how members of a religious tradition use the texts. That's what makes scripture, according to Smith—at the same time, asserting that "probably no one on earth today knows what scripture is or why."[5]

In most religious traditions, authorities within that tradition designate which texts are scripture. Occasionally, a single expert makes the call, but it must be supported by wider acceptance. As much as religions might contend that the decisions on canon were guided by God or based purely in spiritual motives, the very idea that someone is exerting power to make a decision makes the definition of canon a political process. Those who are in power declare one passage holy and another as something else.

Each decision on canon has its own particular history. Rarely does the decision come out of the blue to make a book canonical scripture. Sometimes, scripture is accompanied by stories of how it came from the mouth of God, or how God guided the pen of the writer. Often, such stories grew up around the text long after it came to be accorded scriptural status. Sometimes, these stories themselves become a kind of scripture, like the Islamic *hadith*—accounts of Muhammad's life, including his rulings on various aspects of law or practice—and other kinds of commentary can become canonical themselves.

What usually came first, before the stamp of approval by authorities, was that the religious community had fallen in love with the text. The people read it in ritual, turned to it for inspiration, and recited it as families or congregations. Often, works that were to become scripture were part of the oral tradition for generations before they were even written down, long before any official designation as part of scriptural canon.

At times, the people have resisted religious authorities' declarations and embraced books the leaders had rejected. For example, during the Protestant Reformation, Martin Luther succeeded in setting aside the Apocrypha and removing it from canon, but his arguments to similarly dump Esther, Hebrews, James, Jude, and Revelation from the Protestant canon failed because other Protestants defended them.

Community use of a text, then, shapes and helps decide what ultimately becomes scriptural. Though the dictum of authority has its role, scripture has to have a community endorsement, or it will die. We can study scriptures of cultures and societies that have ceased to exist, but in each case the scripture still has its source and foundation in a particular group of people.

Because they are integral to the life of a community, scriptures change and evolve over time. New translations take the place of old; religious leaders change the canon, as Luther did, cutting some books or chapters out or letting new ones in. New religious sects arise and add to existing scriptures. There's an idea in Western popular culture that scripture is by definition immutable and therefore irrelevant to the times we live in. Traditionalists assert that texts are rigid, unchanging and unchangeable. Study of the history of texts generally contradicts that view.

Bias in Our Views of Scripture

Two contradictory impulses complicate our designation of scripture from cultures other than our own. First is the tendency to universalize, to regard the sacred books of other cultures as functioning exactly the same way as those from our own culture. While overlap exists, each religious tradition has different methods of establishing what is scripture and may not even endorse anything as scripture in a formal way. Scripture doesn't play the same role in all faiths. Protestant Christianity, in particular, focuses on scripture more than on other aspects of religious practice; Martin Luther's words, *sola scriptura* (scripture alone), echo through that tradition. So, we need to ask adherents of a faith tradition how their texts evolved, how they use them, and what the books mean for that particular people.

Religion itself is a concept developed in a particular context—a modern Western context. Some cultures do not separate out religion as we do, or do not draw the same lines between religion and philosophy.

Other Western biases have to be acknowledged in our view of scripture. For example, when Westerners first encountered sacred texts in China, they applied two different terms to the single Chinese word, *ching* (also written as *jing*). They tended to translate it as "scripture" when it applied to Buddhist texts and "classics" when it applied to Confucian texts. The use of those terms became a convention in comparative religion, based on a Western bias.

Not all scripture is the same, nor can we claim some scriptures to be more legitimate than others. To widen our lens requires inclusion of all kinds of *ching*, however it is translated: sacred texts, holy books, scripture—perspectives that often contradict one another. What all share in common is that particular religious communities set them aside as special. We get to explore what others have found special, and perhaps find something special ourselves.

A Reading from the Analects of Confucius

2. The Master said, "The *Odes* are three hundred in number. They can be summed up in one phrase, 'swerving not from the right path.'"
3. The Master said, "Guide them by edicts, keep them in line with punishment, and the common people will stay out of trouble but will have no sense of shame. Guide them by virtue, keep them in line with the rites, and they will, besides having a sense of shame, reform themselves."
4. The Master said, "At fifteen I set my heart on learning; at thirty I took my stand; at forty I came to be free from doubts; at fifty I understood the Decree of Heaven; at sixty my ear was attuned; at seventy I followed my heart's desire without overstepping the line."

> Analects of Confucius, 2:2–4,
> translated by D. C. Lau

"THE MASTER" in the particular text above is, of course, Confucius himself, as quoted by his students. The man Westerners call Confucius was K'ung Chi'iu, or K'ung Fu-tzu. He lived during the fourth and fifth centuries BCE. The Odes (or Shi-Ching) to which he refers also have been called the Classics of

Poetry, and earlier they were called 300 Poems—though there are 305 and they might more accurately be labeled as songs, as they frequently had accompanying music. The book includes folksongs, ritual pieces, and hymns of praise to the Zhou dynasty's founders.

How could K'ung identify such a motley collection as an important ethical guide, as he does in this passage? The Zhou dynasty, central to much of the Odes, held that rulers were entitled to govern based on how well they treated the people. That principle is also core for K'ung, who extols proper relationships including, but not limited to, the relationship of the ruler to the people. The work's inclusion of folksongs from different regions demonstrates that rulers needed and should respect the people. K'ung urges that people be ruled not through fear but by calling them to be virtuous, which he calls having a sense of shame. We might call it developing a conscience.

The passage describes the importance of studying and learning the Odes, or *ching*, as the Chinese people call them. Clearly, the narrator finds them helpful. But are they scriptures? Some scholars use that word, while others stick to calling them classics. However, the *ching* of China are scriptural in that they shape the beliefs and ethics of the people. They set the standard for what a righteous person does and says and provide the foundation for Chinese culture.

Though he and many others regarded the study of certain texts as important, there was not yet a formally designated canon. Nevertheless, K'ung Chi'iu studied and taught these Chinese texts. Tradition credits him with collecting and editing the Five Classics: Classic of Poetry (or the Odes), Book of

Documents, Book of Rites, I Ching, and Spring and Autumn Annals, which, in time, made up the Confucian canon.

In this particular passage, he describes learning through a lifespan, all based in careful study of the classics, particularly the Odes, even though the book was not officially recognized as canon. That designation eventually came from the Han rulers. While no one single moment or decision cemented the Chinese canon, various decisions during the Han dynasty increased K'ung Chi'iu's status. He had been dead for a few hundred years by then, and rulers elevated his title and offered him sacrifices as they did other noteworthy ancestors. At the same time, they denigrated or ignored other teachers. As K'ung's influence waxed, so did that of the books with which he had associated himself. By 136 BCE, the Five Classics were required material for the examinations for governmental officials and remained so until 1905 CE.

In addition to the classics K'ung had collected and edited, his own words taught about virtue, responsibility, and rituals. Compiled by his disciples after his death, the Analects of Confucius, or Lunyu, were at first considered only a commentary on the Five Classics. Gradually, though, as more people studied the sayings, the collection gained status. Because the Analects are simpler than the classics, students learned them as their first texts, a practice that lasted for a millennium and a half after his life. K'ung's work also was designated as one of the Four Books by the scholar Zhu Xi as part of the movement to establish a coherent Chinese canon.

Tragically, K'ung died believing he had been unable to influence his beloved nation. He had served in government, where his efforts weren't fully appreciated. During the chaotic times in which he lived, with warlords striving for influence and territory, his admonitions for just rule and proper relationships stood in contrast to the brutal power-grubbing that seemed to lead to success. He alienated the warlords through insistence on right action.

However, his work did help establish a canon, and K'ung would have been astounded by his deep, lasting influence on Chinese culture, history, government, and religion. Unearthing the history of how the work grew in influence and came to be identified as sacred provides insight into Chinese culture that applies even today.

CHAPTER TWO

Scripture and Authority

. . . But those who are to receive teaching [are] the
living who are inscribed in the book of the living.
It is about themselves that they receive instruction. . . .

The Gospel of Truth 21,
The Nag Hammadi Library,
edited by James M. Robinson

"IT'S IN THE BIBLE!"

This statement is often used to justify a claim or argue a
point by those who see scripture as a stable and reliable source
of values in a time when social mores in the wider culture are
shifting rapidly. On the other hand, many of those who are
hostile to the idea of scripture say that it has been used as a
weapon against their beliefs or identities.

It's easy to assume that scripture inherently requires its
adherents to believe that there is only one possible truth and
that this truth is known. But even a general overview of how
scripture evolved in some traditions shows that some communities encourage a flexibility of interpretation. As the discussion of the Analects shows, the use of certain texts intertwines
with their designation as sacred. The process of canonization

can take hundreds of years, though it may seem to us in retro-spect that it was a momentary judgment.

Beginnings of the Torah

Starting around 1200 BCE, the Hebrew people began to pass along oral traditions. Gradually, scribes recorded the trans-missions of poetry, law, and history. Over time, some writers consolidated texts, producing a single scroll out of separate versions of the same story, or interwove songs or proverbs drawn from separate sources. The scholar Norman Gottwald has compared the development of the Hebrew Scriptures to a huge river system, in which various books emerged, grew together, and sometimes even separated.[6] While the mouth of the river may look like a huge, singular entity, the network of streams, tributaries, and branches that formed it covers a far-reaching area, tremendously complex and hard to map. If we read closely, we can still see the seams of these inter-weavings in the contradictions, repetitions, and changes in the narrative voice of the biblical text.

The Torah—the five books of Moses—was central to Juda-ism by 400 BCE. It's hard to look that far back through the haze of time, but we have hints from the scriptures themselves as to how these books may have been assembled into one collection. The books of Ezra and Nehemiah (see particularly Nehemiah 8) recount the return of the Hebrews, especially their leadership, to Palestine from the Babylonian captivity. The community's recovery included rebuilding of the Temple at Jerusalem, where the books of Moses were re-discovered.

The passage at the end of this chapter takes a closer look at how Nehemiah tells the story.

In the Torah, Genesis, Exodus, and Numbers include foundational stories of the ancestors: Abraham, Isaac, Moses, and other figures. Leviticus and Deuteronomy define the specifics of the law for the Jewish people. Together, these documents forged a connection among the people, a connection centered in rituals carried out in the Temple at Jerusalem. Later, the rabbis would establish the books themselves as a new way to unite the Jews after the Romans robbed them of their Temple and exiled them to distant lands.

At the same time, some of the oral traditions remained oral. Orthodox Jews posit that from the time of Moses, both a written Torah and an oral Torah existed, the oral Torah passing on deeper and more developed understandings of the law. Eventually, the oral Torah, too, would be written.

Gradually, religious leaders added prophetic books, various writings that included the Psalms and Proverbs, and special books that related to particular holidays, such as Esther, always read at Purim, and Jonah, read at Yom Kippur. These provided the fodder for the rabbis to work with as they finalized the Tanakh, or Hebrew Bible, in the first century.

Establishing a Jewish Canon

The first century of the Common Era (CE) was a turbulent time in the Roman province known as Judea, the home of the Jews. The destruction of the Temple in the year 70 changed *all* Judaism radically. Splinter groups abounded. The Pharisees

studied, practiced, and extolled the law as acts of divine worship. The Sadducees, used to keeping up the Temple, struggled
to find their purpose. The Zealots and Sicarii incited revolu-
tion against Rome. The Essenes withdrew from society and
became ascetics.

The Temple had been central to the ritual and identity of
Jews, but especially to those whose roles related to the Temple.
The historian Josephus contended there could only be "One
Temple for One God."[7] However, the One Temple that existed
was not the original temple built by Solomon. Rather, it was
the Second Temple, built in 516 BCE, when the Jews, many of
them the cultural and political elite, returned from the Babylonian exile. There the Jews observed their central agricultural
festivals—Passover, Shavuot (Weeks), and Sukkot (Booths)—
as commanded in the Torah. People sacrificed their doves,
oxen, and goats at the Temple for personal, family, and community celebrations. Even though Jerusalem had been ruled by
foreign powers and the Jews themselves scattered to distant
lands, with concentrations in Egypt and Babylon and sprin-
klings throughout the Roman Empire, the Temple gave Judaism its center.

While militarists continued to fight against Rome, the religious leaders, particularly the Pharisees, decided that a new
way had to be forged. They did not give up hope that the
Temple would be restored, but they thought, even if rebuilt, it
would always risk destruction. The Jews would have to
enshrine their traditions in another way, releasing the Temple
from its priority and turning instead to the study of scripture
and its practices. Returning to the oral tradition they had

begun with, they memorized the Torah and other key texts, fearing the scrolls, like the Temple, could be destroyed. The scripture itself was supplemented by the oral transmission of rulings of the various rabbis. The rabbis believed that they needed to clearly name which texts were to be considered scripture as they refocused the Jewish people on the words to preserve their tradition.

For generations, the Torah had held authority, but what about all the other books? Which were authoritative and which extraneous? Jewish sects disagreed. Different groups cited alternative texts as authoritative. The rabbis were uncomfortable with this chaotic approach and wanted a canon, a list of approved sacred texts from which to derive law and practice.

The rabbis agreed on twenty-four books that were to be considered scripture: the Torah (Genesis, Exodus, Leviticus, Numbers, and Deuteronomy); the Nevi'im (the writings of various prophets); and the Ketuvim, or Writings (histories such as Chronicles, Ezra, Nehemiah, and books of wisdom such as Proverbs and Ecclesiastes). Together, the scripture became known as Tanakh, a contraction of Torah, Nevi'im, and Ketuvim. In the process, the rabbis omitted anything they believed was written after the time of Ezra. Some of these later texts had been included in the Septuagint, the Greek version of Jewish scripture used throughout the diaspora.

What happened to the left-out books? They didn't disappear. Some were later included in the Apocrypha of the Christian Bible. Though the rabbis rejected them as too recent to be scriptural, both Catholic and Orthodox Christians still call them scripture. Other books were lost until the Dead Sea

Scrolls were unearthed in 1947. Are these non-canonical books scripture? Some scholars would say so because certain sects, like the Essenes, lived by them and treated them as scripture. However, the decision-makers among both Jews and Christians rejected them.

Back to the rabbinical decision-making. Shortly after they established the canon, the rabbis started another project to reinforce the centrality of the texts. They wrote down the interpretations they had memorized from their various teachers, producing a Mishnah, which means "learning by repetition," a tribute to how they had learned the teachings that they believed to be passed down from ancient times. Completed by the end of the second century, the Mishnah provided a comprehensive view of the law, including the rabbis' various arguments about it. That was not the last word, though. Adding interpretations and readings of the Mishnah, rabbis in different places created two different Talmuds (the word appropriately means "study"), the Jerusalem Talmud and the Babylonian Talmud, centered in each of those two geographic regions. The Talmud placed the Mishnah at the center of each page and literally filled the wide margins with interpretation and commentary. These works, crucial to rabbinic study, never had the ultimate authority held by the Tanakh, but deeply influenced Judaism by spelling out the specifics of the law.

Not that the Talmud is a boring law journal. Rather, it sprawls through the practices of Judaism, applying a combination of pragmatism and imagination to real and hypothetical issues. Though the Talmud does define and explain the law, the main focus of studying it is simply to better understand the

Torah. A broad collaboration, the Talmud explores questions, shares debates, defines words, struggles with biblical discrepancies, and expresses doubts.

Though the rabbis didn't make final decisions on what was in the Jewish canon until late in the first century, the road to this point was long and circuitous. What's more, the process didn't end, as prominent rabbis such as Maimonides and Rashi continued writing commentary into the Middle Ages. Even today, work goes on in legal rulings, or *halakha*, made by rabbis to respond to questions that couldn't have occurred in earlier times, applying to cars and computers and artificial insemination. The collections of legal rulings are called *responsa*. Though not scripture, they provide significant advice about how Jews, particularly though not exclusively Orthodox Jews, should live their lives.

The Christian Canon

While the rabbis created their canon, Christians had their own process of decision-making. In the middle of the second century CE, the gnostic-leaning bishop Marcion created a crisis for other Christian leaders by proposing a canon that excluded the Hebrew Scriptures, relying exclusively on more recent works—ten of the letters attributed to Paul, plus the Gospel of Luke—all edited according to Marcion's personal idea of truth. He believed that the God of the Hebrew Scriptures was distinct and different from Jesus' Father, so the old works should be rejected.

Marcion's proposed canon stirred fierce repudiation. One of the church fathers, Iraneus, countered with a more comprehensive scripture that included the gospels of Matthew, Mark, and John, in addition to Luke. He also added the Acts of the Apostles, supplemented Paul's letters with those of James, Peter, and John, and capped it off with Revelation and the Shepherd of Hermas. With small modifications (the addition of Hebrews, Philemon, Jude, and a few epistles, and the rejection of the Shepherd of Hermas), Iraneus's suggestions would endure until the canon was fixed, around the fourth century. By then, the Emperor Constantine wanted a definitive book to publish as the New Testament.

Meanwhile, the Church Fathers agreed, against Marcion, that the Hebrew Bible (what they called the Old Testament) was, indeed, canonical—meaning that Christianity was intimately connected in its origins, beliefs, and practices with Judaism. However, they did not agree on which books of the Hebrew Scriptures to include in the canon. Ultimately, some texts were deemed to be deutero-canonical—constituting a secondary canon known as the Apocrypha. The books of the Apocrypha were not written in Hebrew, but in Greek, probably because they were written later. Some believed that made them less authoritative, a decision very similar to the one made by the rabbis in Judaism.

In time, the Catholic and Orthodox churches accepted the Apocrypha, while much later, the Protestants rejected it. Different groups, different scriptures. Accepting scripture as legitimate relies primarily on the judgment of the religious leaders who have the trust of their communities.

Chinese Classics

The Chinese classics include both Confucian and Taoist texts, though there is some overlap. While the Confucian canon is limited, the Taoists include many more texts. Classics in both traditions are almost entirely attributed to particular individuals, though sometimes the authors may be mythic figures. Even when a master produced part of a work, students often completed, commented on, or elaborated the book. With the emergence in the third century BCE of religious Taoism, in contrast to philosophical Taoism, some Taoists came to understand the scriptures as having eternal existence. They believed the works were revealed to the author as eternal texts from Heaven, similar to other traditions that claim God-given books.

We saw something of the development of the Confucian classics in the reading following the last chapter, but to complete the picture, we need to say more about Taoism. Both traditions are ancient in their philosophical underpinnings, and throughout their development they influenced one another. When Buddhism came to China, the three traditions intermingled.

Taoism, though, has its unique set of texts, more comprehensive than the Confucian canon. Most fundamental are the Tao Te Ching and the Chuang Tzu, a couple of the thousands of texts that were not organized until the fifth century CE. Periodically, rulers suppressed certain texts; notable among them was Kublai Khan in the thirteenth century.

Other Eastern Traditions

Though the Bible—Christian or Jewish—contains a number of books, and the Confucian Chinese classics can be assembled on a short shelf, all these collections are dwarfed by the libraries of Hinduism. The Vedas—Rigveda, Yarjurveda, Samaveda, and Atharvaveda—are supplemented by the Brahmanas, Aranyakas, and the Upanishads. Many other texts exist, including the Vedangas, Upaveda, Dharma Shastras, epics (Ramayana and Mahabharata), Puranas (which refer to themselves as the fifth Veda!), Stotras, Agamsa, Tantras, and Darshanas. And that's only what is left; many of the texts have been lost over the centuries. As in other faiths, various sects or schools of thought see the books differently. However, Hinduism has its own particular perspective, one that Unitarian Universalists might recognize some kinship with. Hinduism does not have a canon in the same way Christianity and Judaism do, because authorities tended to accept a greater diversity of thought, even if they chose to ignore particular books in their own teaching. So, all the different perspectives of theology, Gods, stories, and practical knowledge exist side by side.

Teachers are vital in the Hindu tradition and are more central than scripture, which is not expected to speak for itself. For generations the scriptures circulated orally only, so one could only learn the words through a teacher, or guru. Today written texts are available, of course, but a teacher is still seen as the way to access those texts. The teacher must lead the student not only to understand what is written, but even to pronounce words correctly, particularly for the Vedas, which are written in accented Vedic Sanskrit. Bits of scripture are recited in the context of performing prayers or other religious practices, so what has been written is still learned orally, even today. Oral tradition remains a recognized and authoritative source of truth. In fact, the only way to access some inherited traditional customs is through oral instruction.

Scriptural texts are primarily in Sanskrit. While most Hindus speak one of several languages influenced by Sanskrit, and Sanskrit is one of many official languages of India, it is not an everyday spoken language. Of course, scriptures have been translated into many vernacular languages. Still, many people chant the original Sanskrit, as they believe it to carry deeper meaning.

Hindus describe the Vedas as being unauthored (*apaurusheya*), eternal and divine themselves, rather than human works. "Veda" means wisdom or knowledge. Again, like the Hebrew Scriptures and much of the New Testament, the Vedas circulated orally long before they were written down, earlier than 1000 BCE. Some scholars give the date as the Vedic period of Hindu history, 1500–500 BCE. Others say the Vedas come from thousands of years earlier. Certainly, the Vedas predate the religious tradition called Hinduism.

The dating of Hinduism has challenges, though, in part because Hinduism itself is hard to pin down. While Buddhism and Jainism seem to have evolved shortly after the Vedic period, Hinduism as a separate religious tradition may have come even later, despite its foundation in the Vedas and the practices they prescribe, which precede Buddhism and Jainism. That apparent contradiction reflects the complexity and diversity of the Hindu religion. The various religious traditions that grew up on the Indian subcontinent influenced one another, and some ended up under the Hindu umbrella. Others, like Buddhism, did not, a key reason being that Buddhists do not accept the Vedas.

Hindus classify the Vedas as *śruti*: revealed to the sages, heard by them. That is, they are understood to have existed as truths before they were written or recited. Sifting through to discover their origins appears an impossible task. Tradition says that Bhagavan Brahma revealed the Vedas after creating the world. Others say that Brahma, the supreme being, revealed the Vedas directly, either to four particular teachers or to hundreds of teachers. The key is that the Vedas are special, eternally existing and revealed to humanity.

In contrast, the epics (Ramayana and Mahabharata), Puranas, and other works are called *smrti*, meaning "what is remembered." Orthodox Hindus do not question *śruti*, considering it completely authoritative. *Smrti* represents tradition, and such books are likely more familiar to many Hindus. They are a second tier of scripture. *Śruti*, being eternal and uncreated, trumps anything that is only *smrti*. However, significant books, such as the Bhagavad-Gita (which comes from the epic Mahabharata), have the *smrti* label, though not all schools of Hinduism agree on that. Some put the Bhagavad-Gita, the Agamas, and the Divya Prabandham into *śruti*. So not all schools of Hinduism agree on which texts belong in which classification. Then there are all the Hindu devotional writings in various languages of the subcontinent. If the Hebrew Bible is compared with a single river system, the Hindu texts might be compared with the river systems throughout an entire region, much more elaborate, growing, and flowing organically across India.

Some texts deserve special mention. The Agamas, or Tantras, deeply influence the daily practice of Hinduism, particularly in regard to how particular deities are worshipped. Different Agamas pertain to different Gods—for instance, the Vaishnava Agamas address the worship of Vishnu, and the Shaiva Agamas describe Shiva worship. Emerging around the sixth century, the Agamas shaped the practice and thought of Hinduism. Though the Agamas apply only to a particular tradition, some Hindus view them for their tradition as so central to religious practice that they think of them as *śruti*.

The religious texts in Hinduism have not been taught in a linear way. Chant has been the most popular way to learn texts, though the texts are also taught through ritual, music, dance, and, alternatively, through scholarly tradition, carefully preserving the ideas, philosophies, and cosmologies.

Similarly, Buddhist texts originally were passed on orally, and were probably written down several hundred years after the Buddha's death. Tradition contends that Buddhist sutras— the teachings and sermons of the Buddha and his immediate disciples—were compiled orally at the First Council in Rajagrha soon after Buddha's death (probably in the fifth century BCE). Teams of monks committed them to memory. Around the first century BCE, Buddhist monks feared their tradition might not survive as oral teachings passed from teacher to disciple. They began writing down what they had learned. Various Buddhist schools already had grown up, and each wrote its own version, all of them extensive. As Buddhism migrated to new places, others began recording their own versions in their own languages. The Pali Canon has 45 volumes, the Chinese, 100 volumes, and the Tibetan, 325.[8]

Sutras, recognized as coming from the buddhas and bodhi-sattvas, form the core of teachings and were developed the ear-liest. Added to them are *shastras*, investigations and interpretations that came later. Their usefulness establishes their authority; even the Buddha himself said that Buddhism was not based on his own authority but was true because its practices worked.

Words attributed to the Buddha mingle with interpretations added over the centuries, with rituals and other practices, angled in different ways depending on the line of tradition. Various schools disagree about the authority of each other's sutras. As with Hindu texts, some Buddhist texts require the learner to be taught by a recognized authority. Mastering any particular set of scriptures requires tremendous study. No one masters them all.

Though Buddhism was influenced by many of the same sources as Hinduism, Buddhists do not call on Hindu texts in the way Christians draw on Jewish texts. Instead, Bud-dhists rely on their own extensive collections. The texts are considered the closest access to the Buddha himself, or to the Dharmakaya—the body of truth that can manifest in scripture, teachers, or even Buddha bodies. The texts, then, are treated with reverence, often chanted aloud or physically copied as a spiritual practice.

Texts Revealed as One

We have so far considered texts that have been cobbled together across centuries. Other traditions have a single book, revealed to one person, generally depicted as a messenger of God. In these cases, the text usually comes in a mystical experience.

Take, for example, the Qur'an. The Islamic tradition tells the story of how Muhammad, an Arab trader, became prophet of God. Deeply concerned about divisions and violence in Arab society and acquainted with the Judaic and Christian traditions of his era, he practiced prayer and reflection. Once, while Muhammad was on retreat in a cave, early in the seventh century CE, the angel Gabriel came to him and commanded him to "Recite!" or "Read!" (translations and interpretations vary). Muhammad reported he was unable to. That is when Muhammad is supposed to have received his first of many revelations.

Uncertain whether he was mad or mystic, he returned to his wife, Khadijah, who believed in his vision and took him to her cousin, a Christian, who also affirmed the experience. The revelations continued to come to Muhammad for more than twenty years. He taught the revelations verbally to his followers. Some followers wrote down the words they were taught, either during his lifetime or later. Others simply retained them by memory. The third caliph, Uthman, decided that an authoritative text needed to be determined. The process required a team of editors to interview people who had memorized what they had received from Muhammad and to examine the written documents, together producing what's called the Uthmanic text, compiled only a couple of decades after Muhammad's death. In contrast, the Christian gospels took decades longer. The text was arranged not thematically or chronologically, but roughly from the longest *suras* (chapters) to the shortest. This process created the text that came to be the definitive Qur'an.

However, some critics have posited that the Qur'an did not come from a single source as the story tells, but had earlier influences, borrowing from both polytheistic Arab sources and from Christianity, and may not have been fully developed for a couple centuries. Muslims contend that the apparent borrowing comes because God's revelation was in relation to a particular time and place—that of seventh-century Arabian society, where it would have been natural to include references to such knowledge—and that the accounts from the times, as well as analysis of the texts themselves, substantiate the early completion date.

Whatever its actual origins, the Qur'an is accepted by Muslims as both authoritative and sacred in itself. Some have compared its centrality in Islam not to another scripture, but to Jesus himself in the Christian tradition, as the physical revelation of God. Only the original Arabic version counts as the actual Qur'an. Translations don't carry the purity and holiness of the real thing but are mere interpretations. Qur'an means recitation, rather than writing, and that mode of encounter continues to influence how Muslims perceive the Qur'an. For many, it is an aural experience, and even if the hearer does not fully understand the Arabic words, the beauty of the chant inspires and uplifts believers. Having a melodious text revealed to a single person may help account for Muslim faith in the Qur'an.

An indicator of the singular nature of the Qur'an is the way it speaks of itself as more than an example of an authoritative book, and as the pinnacle of such books. Muslims accept that biblical texts also are sacred. The Qur'an itself incorporates some of the teachings of Abraham, Moses, and Jesus but positions itself as the final authority.

If the role of the Qur'an in Islam is comparable to the role of Jesus Christ in Christianity—as the central revelation—then the Hadith functions more like the New Testament. The Hadith (first complied around the eighth century) includes various individual *hadith*: traditions or stories related to Muhammad, the revelations to him, and the early history of Islam. Each *hadith* includes an *isnad*, or assertion of authority based on a *sanad* (chain) of tellers that goes back to Muhammad. Each link of the chain is one person who has been part of the transmission, one who has received the particular *hadith* and passed it on to someone else. Each person in the chain must be reliable if the teaching is to carry authority. Islamic scholars sift and sort the *hadith* to determine the reliability of each. Disagreements are frequent, so there is no well-defined canon of *hadith*, despite the importance of them to Islam. Related but distinct from the Hadith is the Sira, or the biography of Muhammad, which also helps Muslims and non-Muslims better understand the context from which the Qur'an comes.

Islam is not the only religion shaped by a solo mystic. In 1823, a vision of God and Jesus led a teenaged Joseph Smith in Manchester, New York, to a collection of golden plates engraved with words from a foreign language. Then, Smith alone received the ability to translate them into English. Like Muhammad, he did not have much formal education, so the translation was no small matter. Smith accounted for it as a gift from God. The Book of Mormon came from a single source without elaboration but with a mystical experience. Mormons consider the book a revelation of God equivalent to the Christian Bible, which they also revere.

Similarly, the Baha'i people consider works of Baha'u'llah and the prophet who preceded him, the Bab, as revealed by God. Unlike texts from older religious traditions, Baha'i scripture can be fairly reliably traced to particular authors and times.

When the origins of books are less obscure, two opposite reactions occur. They may be viewed as less authoritative because of recent and clearly human origins. On the other hand, if the religious source is highly trusted, the books may be seen as more authoritative because they came from a recognized spiritual source.

Other religious texts have their cultural histories, usually comprised of some combination of books written by a specific prophet or teacher, recordings of oral texts passed down, and elaborate editing. No matter how a religious tradition describes the genesis or development of the holiness of texts, no text becomes scripture without a religious community using and affirming it. Though canonization may prescribe study of texts, it would not occur without people first finding value in the work. Religious traditions offer a wide variety of explanations for why particular texts are recognized as set-apart. The one thread that holds all of these divergent books together is that particular groups of people regard them as special.

Non-Canonical Scripture

Orthodox practitioners might find the term "non-canonical scripture" an oxymoron. If it's not in the canon, it's not scripture, they'd say. Yet many traditions have some quasi-canonical works, like the previously discussed Apocrypha—accepted by some sects and rejected by others. These books, nevertheless, are included in most Protestant Bibles, even though Protestants see them as secondary to the Hebrew Scriptures and New Testament. As confusing as this is, such books are a tiny minority of works we might consider scripture that could be seen as "outside the canon." Hinduism, meanwhile, has a library of recognized but non-canonical scripture.

Many traditionally religious people close their eyes to the political nature of the arguments their forebears had about which writings should be considered scripture. Viewing the texts as the word of God, they trust that the people who touched the texts, wrote them, and defined them did so through their adherence to God's will. Some people believe "word of God" can mean revealed by God through the work of humanity, or divinely inspired. Others take it more literally, believing that each word comes directly from God and, as such, cannot be altered.

In contrast, Unitarian Universalists recognize the human origins of all religious texts. While we acknowledge that humans may be inspired by God, or by their understanding of God, to create—or even to collect or edit—the texts of their tradition, we don't place one book above others, at least not officially. Particular Unitarian Universalists may, indeed, elevate one book over another, but as a religious tradition, we have no stated canon.

The fight that went into defining certain books as "in" and others as "out" fascinates many of us because it is strange to our understandings of how to accord value. We rely much more on our personal affinities. We recognize the political nature of decisions about canon. Unitarian Universalists look skeptically at firm lines drawn between the secular and the sacred, so the idea that certain leaders have set aside particular books, while dismissing others, does not sit well.

During the time that Jewish and Christian scriptures were being established, other sects were active, among them the Valentinians, a sect of the broad category of Gnostics. In those confusing days following the destruction of the Temple, the line between canonical and non-canonical had not yet been drawn. Heretics and orthodox had not been sorted as clearly as they would be in the fourth century. Christian Jews were still going to synagogues, and Gnosticism filtered into various religious groups, including pagan and Jewish groups. No doubt, there were worshippers who perceived these various texts as truthful representations of their own faith. For those people, these texts were sacred.

Even today, we may be intrigued by such writings as the Gospel of Thomas or the Hypostasis of the Archons *because* the church fathers—those in authority—refused to sanction them. After all, doctrines that later would be associated with Unitarians and Universalists were condemned by many of the same church fathers. We wonder whether the same bias that existed against our ideas affected the condemnation of others. What, then, might we discover in these other condemned books that could have meaning for us? Studying those might help to illuminate the connections between theology, power, and justice in our world.

Because not all religions have rigorously defined their sacred texts, readers may be forced to judge for themselves what has power, guided by their knowledge of the religious tradition. As we'll see in chapter 7, Unitarian Universalists recognize that truth can come from a wide variety of sources. That said, being non-canonical, existing outside a particular religious tradition's canon, does not mean a text is worthless. In some circumstances, it might be treated similarly to scripture and have a special potential to reward study.

It's interesting to look at the way Unitarian Universalists regard non-canonical scripture from other traditions in the light of a slowly dawning realization throughout our own history that we have wrongly marginalized certain voices in our communities. Gradually we have incorporated words of wisdom from more women, LGBT people, differently abled people, and people of color into our communal practices and teachings. But we still have a way to go. As this book goes to press, Unitarian Universalists across the nation are deeply engaged in an effort to decenter whiteness in our communal culture, which will inevitably influence which texts come to be important to us as a people.

Unwritten Tradition

Written texts are rare, where existent at all, among aboriginal religions. Yet to say those traditions have no scripture may be inaccurate. What would you call a story memorized and recited for centuries, or a ritual enacted with particular words and gestures, passed on meticulously from one generation to the next, if you do not give it the label of scripture? The Vedas and the Torah, the sutras and Psalms, all were oral long before they were written.

Many religions through time have recognized oral as well as written scripture, especially when preserved carefully by repetition from one teacher to another. While some ethnographic studies report particular rituals, stories, and laws,[9] the bulk of sacred lore of native peoples throughout the world, like those of the ancient people before writing, has been preserved only in the oral tradition, or has been lost. In the early twentieth century, some Native Americans, notably Zitkala Sa (Gertrude Bonnin), a Yankton Dakota, and Hum-is hu-ma or Mourning Dove (Christal Quintasket), Okanogan, 1888–1936, recorded some of their traditional stories.[10] So, in relatively recent times, traditional Native American spiritual systems have become more accessible.

This chapter's reading, though, returns us to a biblical reading that describes how the Hebrew people may have come to know some of their foundational texts. We may not be able to rely on such reports as historically accurate. Still, the connection of a people with text carries emotional truth.

A Reading from Nehemiah

¹All the people gathered together into the square
before the Water Gate. They told the scribe Ezra
to bring the book of the law of Moses, which the
LORD had given to Israel. ²Accordingly, the priest
Ezra brought the law before the assembly, both
men and women and all who could hear with
understanding. This was on the first day of the
seventh month. ³He read from it facing the square
before the Water Gate from early morning until
midday, in the presence of the men and the women
and those who could understand; and the ears of all
the people were attentive to the book of the law.
⁴The scribe Ezra stood on a wooden platform that
had been made for the purpose. . . . ⁵And Ezra
opened the book in the sight of all the people, for
he was standing above all the people; and when
he opened it, all the people stood up. ⁶Then Ezra
blessed the LORD, the great God, and all the people
answered, "Amen, Amen," lifting up their hands.
Then they bowed their heads and worshiped the
LORD with their faces to the ground. ⁷Also . . . the
Levites, helped the people to understand the law,
while the people remained in their places. ⁸So they
read from the book, from the law of God, with
interpretation. They gave the sense, so that the
people understood the reading.

⁹And Nehemiah, who was the governor, and
Ezra the priest and scribe, and the Levites who
taught the people said to all the people, "This day
is holy to the LORD your God; do not mourn or
weep." For all the people wept when they heard
the words of the law. ¹⁰Then he said to them,
"Go your way, eat the fat and drink sweet wine
and send portions of them to those for whom
nothing is prepared, for this day is holy to our
LORD; and do not be grieved, for the joy of the
LORD is your strength."

> Nehemiah 8:1–10, The Hebrew Bible,
> New Revised Standard Version

WHAT IS THE EVENT that this passage refers to? What was this
book that created such an emotional response? Why was this
occasion so significant that it was recorded for the Hebrew
people to remember and reflect on?

Scholars believe the books of Ezra and Nehemiah were put
together sometime in the third century BCE, from separate
memoirs of two Jews: Ezra and Nehemiah. Both men appear
to have been sent to Israel from the diaspora by the Persians to
rebuild cohesion and order among their people. The Persians
made this a common practice in the lands they ruled. They'd
assign a governor who understood Persian ways to an area
where that governor had cultural roots. The idea was to create
a colonial rule that the inhabitants would accept. "He's one of
ours," the Persians expected the people to say, and they'd be
less likely to rebel.

The memoirs of Ezra and Nehemiah were at least a hundred years old when they were redacted—that is, put through

a process of editing and composition. Scholars argue about the dating of Ezra and Nehemiah, generally believing that they didn't live at exactly the same time and not even sure which came first.

What is historically verifiable is that many Jews were scattered from their homeland during the Babylonian captivity in the sixth century BCE. After Persia defeated Babylon, the Jews slowly began making their way back home, as the Persians worked with prominent Jews to rebuild their land, including the rebuilding of the Temple.

Something else was built in this time, though, something that would last much longer than the Temple: the collection that would evolve into the Hebrew Bible. We don't know exactly what book Ezra is said to have read in the passage above. Different translations of the Bible call it different things, including "The Revelation of Moses," "The Law," "Instruction," and, in the Jewish Tanakh, the "scroll of the Torah of Moses." But from what scholars understand about the compilation of the Bible, there was no established canon before this time.

The story is that, as the Temple was rebuilt in the latter days of the sixth century, a scroll was discovered; it had been lost and was now unknown to the people. It turned out to be the law that Moses was said to have written, the first five books of the Bible—Genesis, Exodus, Leviticus, Numbers, and Deuteronomy—known to the Jews as the Torah. This is the book that Ezra is assumed to have read from, which caused the people to break down in tears.

That's the mythos. In reality, this is likely the time when the Bible was created, when various sources were woven together into a single narrative. What the book of Nehemiah tells us, though, is that pulling the law together into a seamless whole and beginning to teach it once more to the people helped to renew their connection to one another. Following the reading of the text, the people begin to celebrate the festivals again and share their feast with all who had nothing. This religious activity cemented relationships across class barriers and brought together the elites, who had been living far away, with the people who had remained in Israel. So the returning exiles were dissuaded from foreclosing on indebted people who had stayed with the land to which the Babylonians had laid waste.

We're not told why the people are crying. In the text, we only hear Ezra, or Nehemiah, or the Levites—it's not clear; maybe all of them—telling the people to quit weeping and carrying on. Are the people repenting because, as they hear the Law, they know they have lived in violation of it? That's one interpretation. Are they, instead, moved because they are hearing the stories and connections to their ancestors that they had set aside while suffering the exile? Everyone had suffered, those torn from their homes and those who stayed in a place that had been devastated. Now they heard the words that connected them to one another and to the people from whom they had come.

Though we come from a different time and place, we might imagine what it would mean to hear teachings that connect the listeners to their ancestors, that remind them of the stories their grandparents had told. No wonder the tears. No wonder the eagerness to readopt old practices and rituals, like Sukkot, also known as the Feast of Booths. That's what they do immediately after this story in the account; they celebrate the festival. The people's tears and their renewed practice tell us that a newly discovered scripture held deep and personal meaning for them.

CHAPTER THREE

Historical-Critical Reading

... I was not born with knowledge, but
being fond of antiquity,
I am quick to seek it.

> Analects of Confucius, 7:20,
> translated by D.C. Lau

ANY LITERATURE or history teacher can tell you that texts are
situated in the place and time they were written. The vocabulary, the genre, the structure, every aspect of a work is influenced by the time and culture of its origin—not to mention
the author. While recent works may meticulously cite dates of
publication, names of authors, and references, ancient works
require detective work to unearth even these basics. That's
what historical-critical reading provides. This approach to
interpretation requires examination of the various aspects of
the works, lining them up with what we know about the culture and times, and from that, learning more about the context. The task reminds me of working a jigsaw puzzle, moving
back and forth between the specific details and the big picture
to formulate theories of how this text came to be, then testing those theories against the text itself, as well as historical

information about when it was written. The historical-critical interpreter posits that knowing as much as possible about how a story, poem, or prayer came to be and where it came from enriches understanding and can help avoid misinterpretation. Most people will never be able to engage a text on their own at this level. However, they can learn from people who have done the close study. Judging the accuracy and reliability of a particular interpretation can be challenging. Many theologians, preachers, and lay students, after extensive reading, find particular experts they rely on to help them grasp the context and development of a scripture.

For readers of scripture who are profoundly skeptical about the notion of text as religious authority, historical reading provides a way into engagement. This approach understands the text as a product of human creativity. This kind of reading actively engages the reader's powers of reason. Many who avoid scripture believe that reading scripture is inherently a passive, even anti-intellectual practice. Historical reading of scripture may well convince you otherwise.

Scholars pursue several lines of inquiry to determine the origins of a text. The text itself may present different ways of using language that indicate different authors. Scholars consider the original texts, where they were found, and how they compare to later versions. They might date them using archaeological techniques, examine them with X-rays, or implement other methods of close study to determine alterations that have been made. Researchers also consider how form and style compare to other documents from the time and culture. They seek out ways the works could have been edited.

Students of biblical historical criticism often read and gather data across traditions (Judaism, Christianity, pagan religions of the Romans, Greeks, and Egyptians, and "heretical" sources like some of the Dead Sea Scrolls), to draw conclusions about where particular pieces came from, what message the author was trying to share, and what might be the historical truth. Besides looking at books of the time, academics delve into the work of archaeologists and historians. Interpretation requires a thorough familiarity with the time and culture of the work.

Historical Reading as Spiritual Reading

When academics first began approaching the Bible in this way, some conservative Christians saw the methods as disrespectful to the texts, believing that the detailed work ignored the overall thrust of a godly message and disrupted the coherence of a text they saw as unified. The critics, they believed, focused on the series of patches, overlooking the beauty of the quilt. Many conservatives felt that to focus on the people who put together the books was antithetical to their conviction that the Bible came from God alone. Other Christians, though, found the contextualization of scripture a spiritual as well as intellectual pursuit. As methods developed over the years, it's interesting to find Jewish scholars like Amy-Jill Levine commenting on Christian scriptures. Texts come alive in different ways through the eyes of different religious cultures and traditions added to the historical dimension.

Origins of Biblical Criticism

How did historical-critical interpretation begin? For centuries, only the most educated people had any access at all to biblical texts. Since Latin was the language of scholarship in the West, the Vulgate Bible, the translation Jerome crafted in the fourth century, stood as authoritative.

Renaissance scholar Desiderius Erasmus, a devoted Catholic, read the texts in the original languages and thought improvements could be made on the Vulgate. He produced a Bible in the early sixteenth century that included both Latin and Greek texts. He believed that to fully understand the book required going back to the original language in which it was written. What's more, he felt ordinary people should have access to texts in their own language, so they could study them. At the same time, he found the original grammar and vocabulary of the written word to shape the meaning important enough that he recommended that students read Hebrew, Greek, and Latin proficiently, and refer back to early scholars to fully understand what they found. Erasmus, though, still interpreted with a heavy layer of Christian theology, whether reading the Christian New Testament or looking at Hebrew texts.

Dutch philosopher Baruch Spinoza took interpretation further. In the seventeenth century, he rejected the idea that Moses had authored the Torah, precipitating his expulsion from the Jewish community when he was just in his early twenties. Moses, Spinoza declared, could not have written a book that recounts his own death. Nor would he have referred to himself in the third person. Instead, he identified the likely author of the Pentateuch as Ezra, who, as we've discussed, helped make the Torah central to the Hebrew people.

Of course, academics had previously noticed the unlikeliness of Moses writing about his own death, but Spinoza took it to the next step and began questioning the authority of the text because of such problems. He went so far as to criticize religious authorities who placed too much weight on the words written on paper, saying in his *Theological-Political Treatise*:

> It will be said that, although God's law is inscribed in our hearts, Scripture is nevertheless the Word of God, and it is no more permissible to say of Scripture that it is mutilated and contaminated than to say this of God's Word. In reply, I have to say that such objectors are carrying their piety too far, and are turning religion into superstition; indeed, instead of God's Word they are beginning to worship likenesses and images, that is, paper and ink.[11]

So began the practice of looking at Christian and Jewish scriptures as texts like other books, works that could be examined for inconsistencies and tested against theories of their origins and histories, a practice that came fully of age in the nineteenth century.

The Nineteenth-Century Challenge

German professor of biblical studies Julius Wellhausen, building on the work of Dutch and French scholars, described in his *Prologue to the History of Israel* (1878) the disparate writing

styles present in Hebrew Scriptures, particularly in the Torah.
The book is sometimes compared to Darwin's *Origin of Species*
in its combination of influence and controversy. The documentary hypothesis, as it was called, developed from the
insight that God had different names in the Hebrew Scriptures.
What's more, the sections that used particular names for God
had other stylistic variations that seemed to be consistent.

Wellhausen identified four different authors, whose works
were combined into what came to be the Torah. They were
designated by letters: J, the Yahwist, who referred to God with
the four-letter Hebrew name YHVH, which some Christians
pronounce as Yahweh (*Jahweh* in German); E, the Elohist,
who called God Elohim; P, the Priestly source most concerned
about ritual matters and genealogies; and D, the Deuterono-
mist, who focused on God's judgment. This documentary
hypothesis shapes biblical criticism to this day.

Preachers and religious leaders blasted the theory. The very
idea of deconstructing a sacred text felt irreverent and scan-
dalous, as it had in Spinoza's time. Wellhausen himself resigned
from teaching prospective ministers because he believed his
theory destroyed their faith.

Science and reason had accompanied religion smoothly
for too long. This well-reasoned approach to religion had
other dimensions. Around the same time that scripture was
being re-evaluated, Darwin's theory of evolution challenged
basic perceptions of how the world and its inhabitants had
come to be. Intellectually, the earth shook under the feet of
religion.

Not all people of faith saw historical-critical theory as disruptive to their relationship with God. Henry Ward Beecher,

the respected preacher of Plymouth Congregational Church in Brooklyn, saw the need for new interpretations:

> If ministers do not make their theological systems conform to the facts as they are; if they do not recognize what men are studying, the time will not be far distant when the pulpit will be like a voice crying in the wilderness.[12]

Unitarians, in particular, already relied heavily on reason and had rejected core tenets of Christian dogma. For them, the new readings of scripture, along with the theory of evolution, brought excitement more than controversy. While more conservative religious groups scrambled to bring the traditions and new research in line, Unitarians adopted a scientific worldview. The argument among Unitarians was never between science and the Bible, but more between scientific rationalism and the role of intuition and other mysterious ways of knowing. By the late nineteenth century, some Unitarians had reasoned themselves away from considering the Bible any more important than many other books, though that was a highly controversial stance.

Universalists, too, had long read the Bible seriously, but with a commitment to reason. In contrast to other religious groups, then, Unitarians and Universalists accepted with hardly a glitch the new understandings and interpretations of scripture. Science, they felt, led them to a deeper truth, even of God. So, a scientifically informed scholarship of the Bible brought them closer to truth, and from there to God.

The documentary hypothesis about various authors composing the Torah inspired similar techniques in other parts of the Tanakh, and the Christian scriptures, or New Testament. The New Testament, composed over a briefer time than the Hebrew Scriptures, began with the letters of Paul, probably written in the fifties CE, some perhaps as early as the forties. The first texts of Christianity arose, then, more than a decade after Jesus' death. Paul probably wrote only seven of the thirteen letters usually credited to him. Unknown authors likely composed them throughout the first century, along with other letters included in the New Testament.

The gospels came along while letters were still being written, with Mark coming first, sometime between 60 and 70 CE. Most scholars cite John as the last gospel, written around 90 CE. None of the books were written by the men to which they are credited. Such attributions were common in the ancient world, associating a book with a particular school of thought by claiming one of its teachers as an author. It also helped to get a book taken more seriously. Whoever put the books together drew on oral traditions, some of which were probably around even while Jesus was alive. Scholars hypothesize that there was a source they call Q (for "*Quelle*," German for "source"), which contained a collection of sayings of Jesus and provided material that was used in Matthew and Luke. Those two gospels also drew on Mark. John seems to have been created from an entirely different set of sources.

Historical Jesus

Since the eighteenth century, some scholars of Christianity and Christian texts have focused on the pursuit of the historical Jesus. The primary evidence of Jesus' life comes from texts of one sort or another, primarily the canonical New Testament as well as the non-canonical Gnostic and other texts discovered in the twentieth century. Independently, Josephus, the Roman historian, did mention Jesus, and Tacitus referred to the execution of Christus. As time has gone by, archaeological evidence has influenced what we know, as well as deeper understandings of the context of the time and place.

The focus on a Jesus of history has come and gone through the years, with three separate "quests for the historical Jesus" commonly identified. The first, in the eighteenth and nineteenth centuries, produced a number of biographies of Jesus and harmonies of the gospels. Though not considered part of the scholarly work, Thomas Jefferson's *The Life and Morals of Jesus of Nazareth* is in the spirit of that search. Jefferson, denying the miracles of Jesus, went through the King James Version of the gospels with a razor and glue in hand and cut out the sections he did not believe were realistic or true, preserving and gluing the parts he believed. The volume he produced is often called "The Jefferson Bible" and has resonated with many Unitarian Universalists, even though Jefferson never formally affiliated as Unitarian.

Humanitarian Albert Schweitzer joined the quest and often receives credit for originating the term because of his 1910 book *The Quest of the Historical Jesus: A Critical Study of its Progress from Reimarus to Wrede*. He also gets credit for ending the first quest, as the upshot of his thorough consideration was that everyone saw pretty much what they wanted to see. He asserted that as we look into the deep well in search of the human Jesus, stripped of myths, we see only vague reflections of ourselves.

It wasn't until the 1950s that a new quest rekindled the search. The latest effort, the Jesus Seminar, controversially used colored beads to vote on the authenticity of various words and acts from the gospels. More than a hundred scholars participated, casting votes with red, pink, gray, and black beads to indicate how likely each scholar believed a particular saying or action was actually by Jesus. The process, easy to lampoon, received criticism on various grounds, but contributed to narrowing the gap between the knowledge of the people in the pew and that of scholars. Though the founder of the seminar, Robert Funk, died in 2005, some of the other Seminar scholars have gone on to consider the historical Paul and early Christianity.

The impossible quest continues, as we desire to know more.

Historical-Critical Reading Outside the Jewish and Christian Scriptures

For liberal religious people who are wary of cultural misappropriation, historical-critical reading of scripture may be appealing as an antidote to shallow and uncontextualized engagement that risks misunderstanding. But critics argue whether scholarly Western approaches can respectfully be applied to texts outside their own religious traditions. There's reason for mistrust. For example, since the days of Peter the Venerable, the twelfth-century Cluny monk who commissioned the translation of the Qur'an into Latin, the Western approach to Qur'anic study was to decry Muhammad as a religious imposter who created a monotheistic Arabic religion out of his familiarity with Judaism and Christianity. Westerners who examined the Qur'an usually had little experience with an Islamic approach to scholarship, which relies a great deal on the Hadith and Sira, or biography, of Muhammad.

A few nineteenth-century European Orientalists, such as Abraham Geiger, Theodor Noldeke, and Ignaz Godziher, attempted analysis of Qur'anic texts. Their assumptions of human agency in production of scripture did not fit neatly with Muslim beliefs, but controversy really exploded when John Wansbrough began employing techniques of Biblical criticism in his work with the Qur'an in the 1970s. He questioned whether the Qur'an was formulated in the short time most Muslims contend that it was. Rather, he believed it came out of the ninth century as a justification for some of the rulings of religious leaders of the day, a view widely disputed by Islamic scholars.

A historical-critical approach to the Qur'an, especially when it is done by non-Muslims and when the conclusions contradict central tenets of the faith, strikes some Muslims as irreverent and condescending, as they often show little regard for the approaches Islam takes to its own tradition. Traditional Islamic scholarship has its own processes that account for many of the same factors as historical-critical approaches. Not long after the Qur'an was established, scholars began studying the verses and other sources to determine which verses came when and where they had been revealed, ultimately dividing them according to whether they were revealed in Mecca or Medina.

Muslim scholars begin their work on contextualizing the rise of Islam with examinations of *sira* and *hadith* literature, considering what they knew of the life and teachings of Muhammad, as well as the reliability of their sources. This systematic examination of texts and testing of historical connections comprises a set of uniquely Islamic practices. The task of verifying the origins and tracing the transmission of the traditions has extensive history. Since early Islam, scholars have examined the *isnad*, or sources attached to particular *hadith*, to verify their reliability, investigating each name in the chain of transmission to consider how trustworthy that person was and how likely it was that she or he knew the person from whom the *hadith* came. That particular practice is only one in the broad variety of Islamic investigation. The *tafsir*, or Qur'anic interpretation, includes disciplines that address historical context, grammar, metaphors, variant readings, the relation of laws to one another, and much more.

Like scholars of Jewish and Christian scriptures, Qur'anic scholars have far more questions than answers. Study and argumentation continue around the context that Muhammad came from, who the Qur'an was intended for, and what texts may have been available to early Muslims who were creating their religion and writing down their scripture. The reading following this chapter comes from the Qur'an and will consider some of its connections to Jewish and Christian scriptures.

Meanwhile, the breadth and number of texts of Hinduism and Buddhism and the question of colonialism create challenges for the use of historical-critical interpretations in those traditions. As Westerners took control of Asian lands, they wanted to explore the religious traditions they found and brought their own tools of study to them. Because Europeans had the power, actual practitioners of the religion found them-

selves in a subsidiary position in relation to their own sacred
books.

In Hinduism, textual study by Westerners began in the
nineteenth century. However, they generally neglected the real
religion as lived by actual people. Early historical-critical study
tended to be by Westerners who did not fully understand the
culture, and sometimes even the language, of the texts. As
time has continued, Western scholars have developed deeper
understandings of cultural context and the lived religion,
while Asian scholars have learned Western methodologies.
Controversy about insider and outsider status pervades discussion of the study of Hindu texts to this day. Swami Tyagananda
of the Vedanta Society of Boston has summarized it this way:

> The distinction between intellectual understanding and
> spiritual experience—or "indirect" knowledge (*paroksha-
> nubhuti*) and "direct" knowledge (*aparokshanubhuti*)—is
> often stressed in the Hindu tradition. I feel that keeping this
> distinction in mind is useful for both scholars as well as
> practitioners. Intellectual understanding is important and
> often a necessary prerequisite to spiritual experience, but
> it cannot replace spiritual experience. So both scholars
> and practitioners have something unique to contribute and
> they can be allies in a quest for greater knowledge and
> understanding.
>
> In order for that to happen, the academy as well as the
> practicing community will have to shed their biases. . . .
> The academic study of Hinduism will become richer if an
> effort is made to look at the subject from all perspectives,
> the insider's as well as the outsider's, without privileging one

over the other. Hindu practice will become richer if it gets the benefit of newer ways of approach and newer insights from different viewpoints. No matter what, some differences will persist but bitterness need not.[13]

With an increased understanding of the problems of applying interpretation techniques cross-culturally, historical-critical methods have been applied to texts of Hinduism, Buddhism, Confucianism, and Taoism. The chronology of these scriptures has been established, derived by analyzing the texts in relation to one another and to Chinese historical records. The chronology of texts is understood in the broad sweep of history. Hindu scholars, for example, speak of phases or periods: the Prevedic, the Vedic, the Ascetic (or Classical), the Epic and Puranic, and the Modern. With periods encompassing centuries, precision may be lost. Remember, too, the vast number of texts from across a huge continent. Developing in-depth knowledge of the languages, cultures, histories, and traditions in order to foster deep historical-critical understandings creates challenges. For example, the ancient form of Sanskrit in which the Vedas are written includes some words whose meaning is now completely lost.

Yet, the work goes on. Particular texts have been analyzed with historical-critical tools, and arguments among specialized scholars fill journals and the web. What's more, as actual practitioners of the various religious traditions become versed with historical-critical tools and scholars outside the traditions improve their understandings of the cultural milieu, the study is bound to deepen and yield richer insights.

A Reading from the Qur'an

1. *Alif. Lam. Mim.* 2. God, there is no god but He,
the Living, the Self-Subsisting. 3. He sent down
the Book upon thee in truth, confirming what was
before it, and He sent down the Torah and the
Gospel 4. aforetime, as a guidance to mankind.
And He sent down the Criterion. Truly those who
disbelieve in the signs of God shall have a severe
punishment. And God is Mighty, Possessor of
Vengence. 5. Truly naught is hidden from God on
earth or in Heaven. 6. He it is Who forms you in
the wombs however He will. There is no god but
He, the Mighty, the Wise. 7. He it is Who has
sent down the Book upon thee; therein are signs
determined; they are the Mother of the Book, and
others symbolic. As for those whose hearts are
given to swerving, they follow that of it which
is symbolic, seeking temptation and seeking its
interpretation. And none knows its interpretation
save God and those firmly rooted in knowledge.
They say, "We believe in it; all is from our Lord."
And none remember, save those who possess
intellect.

Qur'an 3:1–7, translated by Seyyed Hossein Nasr

THE ARRANGEMENT and format of the Qur'an is likely to surprise many who are more familiar with linear narration. As
noted previously, the *suras*, or sections, are arranged basically
from longest to shortest. Often, they contain a mixture of revelations from Mecca and those from Medina; those origins are
delineated in some modern copies of the Qur'an. Like the
Hebrew and Christian Bible, the Qur'an includes laws, warn-
ings, parables, prayers, sermons, and narratives. However, the
style is unique. Narratives do not so much tell a story as they
remind the reader of an already known story, referring to it and
describing it. The Qur'an also is more self-referential than
many other texts, describing within the text itself how it is to
be read and understood.

The passage quoted above is called Al-'Imran, or the House
of 'Imran, usually understood to be the family of Mary, mother
of Jesus. That's a hint at the Qur'an's acceptance of elements
of Christianity. What's more, this text explicitly names the
Jewish Torah and the Christian Evangel (or Gospel) as sent
from God as guides for human beings. The Qur'an frequently
refers to Moses, Abraham, Mary, Jesus, and other Jewish and
Christian figures. Early Christian critics of Islam used those
references to criticize the Qur'an as derivative, but Muslims
assert that God sent different revelations to different people
and that God would naturally refer to his other revelations
in the ultimate or final disclosure—the Qur'an. The *hadith*, too,
describe how Jewish rabbis, Christian monks, and even Arab
soothsayers had predicted the coming of Muhammad and his
messages from God.

The *sura* begins with the *muqatta'at*, or abbreviation, "*Alif
Lam Mim.*" This particular combination of letters appears at

the beginning of twenty-nine *suras*, while others start with different mysterious letters. The abbreviations written as a word are sometimes translated as particular attributes of God. Other explanations pop up as well; maybe they are the initials of the transcriber, or perhaps they are only sounds without meaning. Many scholars, though, claim they are best left as something to be understood only by God.

They are an appropriate prelude to a key message found in this passage, which speaks about the Qur'an itself. Some of its verses, it says, are "precise," or clear, unambiguous, without any need for interpretation in order to be understood. Others, though, leave room for interpretation because they are "ambiguous." The text warns the reader that people who are insincere or "wayward" will find ways to make mischief and seek divisions in the community through their interpretations. No doubt such misreading, deliberate or accidental, has occurred with the Qur'an throughout its history, as it has with other holy books.

What guidance, then, is given for interpretation? Very little. Only the assertion that God alone knows how to read those difficult passages. This has led Muslim scholars to classify verses according to how easily they can be interpreted, as either *muhkam*, clear and explicit, or *mutashabih*, hard to understand or with multiple meanings. Law and moral commands often fall under *muhkam*, while attributes of God and God's relationship to the world are often considered *mutashabih*. Scholars suggest the ambiguity of these verses is deliberate, to encourage people to use care whenever they contemplate such theological matters.

Given the challenge of interpretation, Muslim scholars require a range of knowledge to suggest meaning for the more difficult divisions, whether *sura*, verse, word, or even letters. No wonder such an immense range of disciplines have developed that are devoted to coaxing out the meaning of the Qur'an. And no wonder consensus has been so hard to establish for the interpretation of some parts of the texts.

Typical of the Qur'an, the message of this particular passage is embedded in praises for God. The meaning of the Qur'an is said to boil down to the greatness of God. After all, "nothing is hidden" from God, no matter how obscure meanings may be to humanity. This passage reminds me that facile interpretations of the Qur'an, whether they come from fundamentalist Christians determined to condemn the book, or from Islamic jihadists finding inspiration for terrorism, diminish the real complexity of a book deeply valued by more than a billion people throughout the world.

CHAPTER FOUR

Contextual Criticism

Rabbi Birayim said in the name of . . . Rabbi
Bena'a: There were twenty-four interpreters of
dreams in Jerusalem. One time, I dreamed a dream
and went to each of them to interpret it. What one
interpreted for me the other did not interpret for
me, and, nevertheless, all of the interpretations
were realized in me, to fulfill that which is stated:
All dreams follow the mouth of the interpreter.
                    William Davidson Talmud, Berakhot 55B

HISTORICAL-CRITICAL reading provides insights into where
texts came from and how they have been used—but it has its
limits. The approach rose out of Enlightenment thinking,
which valued reason and objectivity. Enlightenment scholars
searched for *the* truth, certain that such a reality existed.

What if truth, particularly of a religious nature, is not completely objective, but dependent on the angle from which it is
seen? This is an idea that is central to Unitarian Universalism.
Indeed, we often say that each person's religious truth is only
one piece of a larger truth that can't be fully known. We have
even dared to claim doubt itself as holy, an essential part of the

59

free and responsible quest for meaning that we affirm in our Principles. While nineteenth-century scholars had noted the different points of view within scripture itself, they sought to understand it without considering that they, too, brought a point of view. They insisted that they could be objective. In the middle of the twentieth century, philosophers and theologians came to see how elusive objectivity really is. Every reader has a point of view, whether or not it is acknowledged. We can be more thoughtful and understand more deeply if we know the perspective of the teller of the story, and the perspective of the intended reader and the interpreter. We might even find ourselves closer to truth if we listen to a variety of readers and interpretations.

Authoritative sources, including but not limited to scriptural texts, often focused on the stories and truths of those people in a society who have power. Consciously and unconsciously, scripture has been used to perpetuate particular viewpoints, endorsing the status quo of power arrangements or shoring up support for someone seeking power. What's more, so has the interpretation of that scripture. Those without power—that is, the majority of people—have been left out of the story and even out of the interpretation of the story. Our relationship to scripture is sometimes formed by early experience in which scripture was used as a weapon of oppression. It is, however, our understanding that no individual has a special claim on the objective meaning of scripture that empowers us to undermine abusive readings and reclaim scripture as a spiritual resource.

Particular criticism of scholastic objectivity has come from people with less power: people of color, women, people who have been colonized, people with disabilities, queer people. In religious studies, these less powerful people have created liberation and contextual theologies. Despite uniqueness in each particular strand, these theologies share an approach that comes from the experience of oppressed people. They draw on sociology and power analysis, politics and history. Most particularly, they draw on the personal experiences of people whose stories and knowledge often have been ignored, disbelieved, or even condemned. Contextual theologies encourage people living with oppression to read texts searching for images of themselves and to criticize how the texts have been used against them. Reception history—the study of how texts have been interpreted over time—plays a role in this process. The goal is to discover and empower the self within a particular identity, leading to liberation from the diminished images that have been presented by an oppressive culture—and maybe even to salvation through shared social action spurred by new insights into old stories.

Though criticized at times as "ideological theologies," liberationists and other contextual theologians would argue that *all* readings, *all* theologies, come from a perspective, an ideology. Biblical scholarship, then, has come traditionally from a particular point of view, a white Western Christian male-privileged point of view. Even those scholars who were not themselves white, Western, Christian, and male have accepted the assumptions that came from that viewpoint in order to be taken seriously in scholarship. Liberation and contextual theologies say yes, you have a point of view, and so do we! None of us is objective. Now it's time to hear what we have to say.

Liberation and contextual theologies demand that those engaged in study, regardless of their personal status, their educational attainment, or their charisma, be accountable to a community of people who experience oppression, whether through colonization, racism, classism, sexism, heterosexism, or other subjugation. They must stay in covenantal relationship with a particular community, in dialogue. Most of those who practice a particular contextual theology also have learned from members of other oppressed groups to take care in doing theology so that they do not exclude, belittle, or marginalize others. Many people are oppressed in one way, while having privilege in others. For example, a gay, white, cisgender man retains both male and white privilege, but encounters oppression due to his sexual orientation. A disabled, Native American, straight, cisgender woman has privilege due to her sexual orientation, but faces oppression in multiple areas of her life. Theologians use various words such as intersectionality, kyriarchy, and domination systems to describe this situation of layers of privilege and oppression.

Keeping various perspectives in mind can be challenging. Communication among different groups deepens everyone's understanding, though. Womanist (African-American women) theologians, for example, have called out white feminists on their racism and called out black liberation theologians on their sexism. Dialogue across these various fields helps make individuals aware of each other's perspectives.

The goal of any of these readings is more than new insights about old stories; it's also about changing society and the use of power in society. Old stories, then, are recast by looking at them from a different point of view, where they can inspire action to bring about change.

No matter the outside communication, contextual theologies rest in a particular identity, with individual writers and speakers bringing insights enlightened by the specifics of the experience that comes from their identity. Identity affects their reading of scripture. Practitioners of contextual theology name their own personal social and political location, acknowledging the identities that shape how they interpret what they read. This is the antithesis of an "objective" point of view, which ignores the viewpoint of the writer who claims an impartial perspective that comes without any personal identity. Rather, contextual theology comes from a fully grounded, specific point of view. Often, through the late twentieth and into the twenty-first centuries, oppressed groups have turned to reading scripture in particular ways as a resource in reclaiming their own identities from their oppressor. It also can be a way to reclaim scripture itself as personally relevant and not bound by the claims made on it by those in power.

Liberation Theology

In the 1950s and 1960s, Latin American thinkers began to articulate how their economic development had been diminished by political and economic colonization by European and North American states. Their religious response was to form base ecclesial communities—groups of poor Catholic people reading scripture together and looking for how it played out in

their own lives. Doing theology themselves, they found empow-
erment through a God who loved them and called them to
resist the oppressive systems in which they found themselves.
Theology, then, came about as a way of describing what was
going on in people's lives, so that it rose from the grassroots
rather than the academy. Eventually, many scholars discovered
this grassroots "liberation theology" when Gustavo Gutiérrez,
a Peruvian Dominican priest of mixed Spanish and Quechua
heritage, summarized key points in A *Theology of Liberation* in
1973. Gutierrez embraced the Marxist idea that thought comes
out of practice. Normal people, even peasants, could gather,
read the Bible, and share stories of their lives. In that way, they
did theology, finding their own lives as sites of God's action,
and looking for biblical inspiration to bring change.

Gutiérrez, often credited as the founder of liberation theology, though he might be better seen as the articulator of it,
speaks of three kinds of liberation: freedom from all forms of
social, political, and economic oppression; recognition that
suffering comes not from God but from human and historical
injustice; and, finally, redemption through the death and resurrection of Jesus Christ. Liberation theologians like Gutiérrez encourage people to ask of scripture: "What does this say
about *us?*" and "Where is God (or Jesus) in this moment and
place?"

In working with these questions, liberation theologians
insist on God's universal love—in which everyone, regardless
of color, heritage, education, class, or economic status, is
included. However, God's preference—a preference Christians
should emulate—is for the poor, those who most need God's
love. Church should be not "for" or even "with" the poor, but

"of" the poor. Those who suffer should make up the church and do its work of liberation.

The movement has been thoroughly grounded in scripture, with the words of the prophets and Jesus' sermon in the field from Luke providing special encouragement and support in liberation theology.

Black Liberation Theology

"If [God's] love was so great, and if He loved all His children, why were we, the blacks, cast down so far?" asks James Baldwin in *The Fire Next Time*, in 1963. Three years later, a group of black pastors bought a *New York Times* ad arguing for black power that found its inspiration in the Bible.

James Cone, often named as the founder of black liberation theology, established both scripture and black experience as key to his explorations. "I knew that before I could say anything worthwhile about God and the black situation of oppression in America I had to discover a theological identity that was accountable to the life, history and culture of African-American people," he claims.[14] But scripture was foundational, too. He looked particularly to the story of Exodus, long claimed by African Americans through music and liturgy, as resonant with the experience of freedom from slavery and transition to a new land. Like the Latin American liberationists, though, Cone found Jesus' life and death to be an affirmation of God's preference for oppressed people over the powerful. He went so far as to say that a God who sided with the oppressed could not be identified with the oppressors. God, then, must be black:

The black theologian must reject any conception of God which stifles black self-determination by picturing God as a God of all peoples. Either God is identified with the oppressed to the point that their experience becomes God's experience, or God is a God of racism. . . .

The blackness of God means that God has made the oppressed condition God's own condition. This is the essence of the Biblical revelation. By electing Israelite slaves as the people of God and by becoming the Oppressed One in Jesus Christ, the human race is made to understand that God is known where human beings experience humiliation and suffering.[15]

Black liberation theologians find God's preferential option, again, with those who live under oppression and seek freedom through their study of God's story in scripture.

In a similar vein, Vine Deloria Jr. (Lakota) titled his 1974 definitive work on Native American religious views *God is Red*.

Feminist Theology

The role of women has been culturally constrained throughout history in most of the world. That means that scripture has often ignored or diminished women's status—or their very being. Catholic feminist theologian Elizabeth Schüssler Fiorenza has recommended what Paul Ricoeur calls a "hermeneutic of suspicion" when reading texts, particularly the gospel stories. By that, she means a technical theological way of reading between the lines, looking with suspicion on what has been written, and considering who did the writing, why, how they were using their power to define truth, and what they are likely to have left out or misrepresented. For example, there would be no need to declare that women could not speak before an assembly unless they were already doing so. This approach invites the reader to consider what might have been happening to cause people in power (men), who had the ability to write books, to make such declarations.

Men, in a society that was often sex-segregated in both roles and socialization, would have omitted automatically stories about women. They might not have known those stories and, if they knew them, would have been acculturated to dismiss such narratives. Many women are included in gospel stories without names or personal identities: the woman at the well, the hemorrhaging woman, the woman caught in adultery. Several women, though, achieve some prominence in gospel texts: Mary, the mother of Jesus; Elizabeth, the mother of John the Baptist; Mary and Martha, Lazarus's sisters; Mary Magdalene; Salome, the mother of James and John. Not as numerous or as high-profile as the men, these and other women must have had an unusual level of notoriety in order to be mentioned at all in the gospels because of men's natural tendency to disregard them. Women play especially crucial roles in the crucifixion and resurrection stories. Chances are, if the men composing these books felt it necessary to include the women, they were even more significant than the stories indicate. (Much the same could be said of the appearances in scripture of any marginalized people.)

The Bible is not the only religious book to slight women. Given the male-dominated cultures from which these books arose, this is no surprise. Hindu texts celebrate the divine as feminine as well as masculine, but this theological equality of the genders does not translate to equality socially or in the family within the religious codes. Both Buddha and Muhammad are credited with having a more open and positive approach to women than most men of their times. Still, Buddha instructed women to obey their husbands, while men should respect their wives; clearly, the husband is the head of the family. Muhammad detailed rights of inheritance and divorce for women, extending and protecting their roles, but did not go as far as we might like in today's world.

Scriptures of more recent faiths, such as Baha'i and Christian Science, have more modern approaches to inclusion and respect for women. However, as a general rule, applying Schüssler Fiorenza's suspicion can help. All traditions have women who exerted influence, whether we know their names or not; women sages in the Rigveda, Gargi Vachaknavi in the Brihadaranyaka Upanishad, Muhammad's wives Khadija and Aisha in the Qur'an, and the judge Deborah in Hebrew Scriptures are examples. Investigating the works of contemporary women and feminist scholars within particular faith traditions can help broaden our understanding of scriptural books and challenge our imagination to help understand women's roles.

Queer Theology

Queer theology developed by building on the critique of gender roles formulated by feminist theologians and the emergence of queer theory in sociology. The theology embraces a view of sexual identities as socially constructed, and it examines the effects of scriptural texts on societal norms and expectations.

From the earliest days of gay pride, activists realized that religious opposition was among the greatest obstacles to LGBT acceptance. People who took both religion and equality seriously began to look for the scriptural challenges and disarm them. "The clobber passages," a handful of Biblical verses primarily from the Hebrew Bible, had long been used to condemn homosexual relations. LGBT readers, as well as straight and cisgender supporters, found new ways of reading and interpreting these passages, or put them into a context where their meaning changed because of better understanding of the culture from which they came. At the same time, they began a quest to find in Hebrew and Christian scriptures depictions of people who might be considered queer: King David's love for his friend Jonathan, the Ethiopian eunuch converted to Christianity in Acts, Jesus' "beloved disciple" John.

These early efforts in the 1970s and 1980s were often labeled as gay or lesbian theology. It wasn't until the 1990s, however, that queer theology fully emerged with a more forthright critique. Queer theologians did not limit their consideration to texts that address gender and sexuality. After all, we do not think about gender and sexuality the same way that people did 2,000, or even 200, years ago. Instead, they took it a step further by applying a queer reading to all scripture, embracing non-traditional gender identities and rejecting binary thinking about sex, gender, and sexuality. While based in reaction against oppression, queer theology goes further to claim the sacredness of queer identity and invite a critical look at all forms of traditional interpretation.

As slam poet J. Mase III says, "You've been lying about my people for too long."[16] Queer theology, like other contextual and liberation theologies, exposes the lies and claims an affirmative identity. Reading scripture can be a radical act to embrace the idea that each person is sacred and loved by God, exactly as they are, even if the culture gives an entirely different message.

A Reading from Luke

Now as they went on their way, he entered a certain village, where a woman named Martha welcomed him into her home. She had a sister named Mary, who sat at the Lord's feet and listened to what he was saying. But Martha was distracted by her many tasks; so she came to him and asked, "Lord, do you not care that my sister has left me to do all the work by myself? Tell her then to help me." But the Lord answered her, "Martha, Martha, you are worried and distracted by many things; there is need of only one thing. Mary has chosen the better part, which will not be taken away from her."

Luke 10:38–42, The Bible,
New Revised Standard Version

LIKE NEARLY EVERY New Testament passage, different readers through the centuries have found various interpretations of the story of Mary and Martha. Since the time of the church father Origen in the third century, though, many readers have understood the story as an admonition to embrace contemplation over action, reflection over doing. This is one of just three short stories in the New Testament that use their names. They show up as friends and supporters of Jesus in both Luke and John, two very different gospel accounts. Tradition has much more to say about Mary and Martha than scripture does.

Interestingly, tradition depicts Martha as the householder, even though she had a brother Lazarus, and also names her as an ordained officer of the early church. She was likely one of the funders of Jesus' ministry, and ancient stories tell of her fierceness. Medieval folklore even credited her with slaying a dragon.

Mary, too, has millennia of myth surrounding her. Traditional stories have grown up in different branches of Christianity, particularly among Catholics and Eastern Orthodox. Who is this Mary? Is she Mary Magdalene, as some claim? Is she the unnamed woman who anoints Jesus in the gospel of John? Some Catholic tradition describes her as an evangelist, converting people to Jesus by telling about how he raised her brother from the dead, as described in the book of John. Cutting through the accretion of legends and speculation is a daunting task.

Applying a feminist lens, a few key points emerge from the brief scripture. First, Martha welcomes Jesus into her home— not her brother's home, not her family's home, not her parents' home—*her* home. This is where the idea of her as the householder comes up. If Martha is a woman with her own home in first-century Palestine, she has significance. She stands out as a model of someone not subordinate to a male, a father or husband, as we might expect in that time and place. Martha presents us with a kind of independence that surprises us in its cultural context, or what we believe to know about the cultural context. Until recently, little research has focused on the role of women in Judaism and its various strands in the first century.

This brings into question some of the assumptions that interpreters have made about Jewish society of the time. There seem to have been Jewish women who stepped outside patriarchal familial expectations, and Jewish men who respected them.

Among those men was Jesus. It's important we not see Jesus as unique in his treatment of women, lest we inadvertently fall into the anti-Jewish bias often associated with Christian interpretation, a bias brought to our attention by Jewish feminist scholars like Judith Plaskow and Amy-Jill Levine. Jesus associates directly with Martha and her sister Mary, not going through any male intermediary. And there is no comment on that in the scripture, so perhaps it was not as unheard of as we have been taught to think it was.

Next, Mary sits at Jesus' feet. Our modern eyes might interpret this as exhibiting a subordinate relationship. However, there's more to it. The stance has particular cultural meaning, showing that she is student and he is teacher. So, Mary's seat at Jesus' feet tells us that she, just like any of his male disciples, has a recognized role as his pupil, his follower—indeed, as his disciple. Mary is depicted as learning directly from Jesus in this passage, while few of the twelve recognized male disciples besides Peter, James, and John get this much ink in the gospel descriptions. The stories of the disciples, except for the initial call stories and the Last Supper, rarely name the more obscure disciples, much less show them in the posture of student in direct conversation with Jesus.

What, then, is "the better part," which Mary has chosen? Patriarchal readings of the passage have argued that Mary was in contemplation, as early church father Origen suggested. The traditional reading contrasts Martha's active service to Mary's contemplative service. But what else might be going on? If Mary was actually a student of the rabbi Jesus, engaged with the teachings of this radical prophet, she may have been preparing for her own active role as teacher and evangelist. Could she have been more actively engaged than traditional readings suggest?

Jesus' affirmation of Mary's role as disciple over Martha's worry about "tasks," which most certainly would have been "women's work," may suggest a proto-feminist endorsement of a woman taking on what could look like a male role—disciple—over her culturally expected completion of household chores. We have to take care in this interpretation, though, because we don't want the passage to be read as women achieving salvation through giving up their femaleness.

Could Jesus have been calling these women to let go of the roles assigned to women and to move where their hearts and minds drew them? To what degree was Jesus stepping outside the parameters of his culture, and to what degree was he part of a countercultural movement within Judaism that called for a change in relations between the sexes? These are only a couple of the questions raised by a feminist reading of the Lukan text.

CHAPTER FIVE

Scripture in Spiritual Practice

The Shabad [sacred hymn] is the Guru, upon
whom I lovingly focus my consciousness;
I am the chaylaa, the disciple.

> Adi Granth, Ramkali Sidh Gosti 943 (Sikh)

A POPULAR MISCONCEPTION is that scripture is all about
what to believe, but religious tradition must be lived. In fact,
in many traditions there's an intimate relationship between
scripture and religious or spiritual practice. The relation of
scripture to practice is complex, though. Scripture guides its
adherents to specific spiritual practices, but it may also be part
of the practice, either through reading, chanting, or praying of
the scripture or through veneration of the text. Many practices
are communal, performed in gatherings of adherents in sacred
space.

Also, many religions encourage individual devotional work:
reading scripture, engaging in private prayer, performing rituals, and divination.

There is a special power in practices and rituals that are
derived from ancient scripture, because they connect their practitioners to generations of history and culture, to a community

of belief and values that traces its lineage back to an original revelation passed down and continuously revered through the ages. In this way, scriptural spiritual practice transcends the individualism that is often the hallmark of modern conceptions of spirituality, especially in liberal religions like Unitarian Universalism. It brings an individual's personal spiritual development into connection with a story and a calling that are much larger than one person's concerns.

Practice or Ritual?

What adherents of a religious tradition call their regular practice may be described as ritual. Religious liberals have, at times, had an uneasy relationship with ritual. Sometimes we have rejected familiar ritual, practices in which we have taken part either as children or as unwilling participants, having experienced it as boring or pointless. At the same time, we find unfamiliar ritual baffling. Unless we study the cultural and religious ground from which it emerges, we cannot begin to comprehend it.

Esteeming critical reason need not contraindicate participation in ritual. The more we learn of how the brain works, the more we understand why humans have come to develop rites and ceremonies that can create communal unity and individual tranquility. Scientific evidence is mounting that ritual improves performance and state of mind.[17] From working through grief to facing an anxiety-provoking situation, ritual can help.

Too often, we have confused ritual with ritualism. Most religions object to ritualism, which holds the performance of ritual as more important than living ethically. (This is analogous to a concern about literalism in reading scripture—that it values the expression more than the intent.) As Confucius said in the Analects, "What can a man [*sic*] do with the rites who is not benevolent?" Similarly, Islam, which has ritual prayers five times each day, cautions those who pray: "Woe to those that pray and are heedless of their prayers, to those who make display and refuse charity." (Sura 107:6–7)

Rituals in Scripture

Across traditions, revered texts spell out rituals. There are the temple sacrifices for the Hebrew festivals of Pesach (Passover), Shavuot (Weeks), and Sukkot (Booths). The bathing of Hindu deities. The various rituals for the Muslim *hajj*, or pilgrimage to Mecca. The use of tobacco in Lakota ceremony. The Christian Eucharist, or Lord's Supper. There are bathing, baptism, and bowing, fasts, feasts, and festivals, sacrifices and offerings, and rites of passage. All these and more get attention in texts that are held as sacred.

Religious ritual takes many forms, not all of which are scriptural. Particular religious texts are associated with rituals, though, or forms of spiritual practice. A physical scripture may be included in a ritual, such as the Jewish practice of standing for and kissing the Torah scrolls as they pass, or dancing with them on the holiday of Simchat Torah at the end of Sukkot. Often, a group of adherents recites, sings, or chants a text together. Sometimes, scripture dictates specific ritual actions. The point is to give oneself over to a practice. In some traditions, such as Islam, this means surrender to God. In others, the goal is to change the individual practitioner. For example, Buddhists use ritual to let go of the ego so that the heart opens, enabling realization and release of delusions as one works toward enlightenment. Rituals are one type of *upaya*, or skillful means, in Buddhism. Engaging in them helps the practitioner.

Ancient Egyptians created the Book of the Dead, which was buried with the dead because its written words, hieroglyphs, were believed to secure protection. Besides describing Egyptian beliefs and customs about death and afterlife, these texts held sacred power in and of themselves to assist the dead in navigating what was to come. Similarly, the namesake Tibetan Book of the Dead, also called *Liberation Through Hearing During the Intermediate State (Bardo Thodol)*, provides instructions to dying or recently dead Tibetan Buddhists so they can overcome the cycle of birth and death. The practice is to read it aloud to the dying person to guide them through the physical and spiritual transition.

Rituals can be a freely offered act of service to one's god. They may target a particular god to urge attention to the adherent's desires. Another idea about ritual is that it actually affects a change, without mediation of the god. This formulaic approach is sometimes labeled magic, or by contemporary neo-pagans, magick.

Significantly, though, practitioners often value the effects on participants in the ritual as highly as, or even more highly than, the effects on the world. Aleister Crowley, whose thinking greatly shaped neo-paganism, wrote about this effect in *Magick, Book 4*:

One must find out for oneself, and make sure beyond doubt, *who* one is, *what* one is, *why* one is. . . . Being thus conscious of the proper course to pursue, the next thing is to understand the conditions necessary to following it out. After that, one must eliminate from oneself every element alien or hostile to success, and develop those parts of oneself which are specially needed to control the aforesaid conditions.[18]

Such intensive personal work as guided by scripture is meant to equip religious people from a variety of traditions to improve themselves.

Communal Prayer

Praying together may be the simplest form of ritual practice. Many scriptures dictate set prayers. At least three times a day, observant Jews refer to the *siddur*, or prayer book, for daily prayers, many of which are taken from the Torah, prophets, and Psalms. Geographic, ethnic, and denominational variations have created a host of different *siddurim* (plural of *siddur*). Some include prayers reserved for the Sabbath, while others offer daily prayers. The Talmud requires a *minyan*, a quorum of ten people (males only for Orthodox Jews) for certain prayers. Offering prayer together creates a different energy than solo prayer. Jewish tradition claims that prayers offered corporately have a more direct route to God. Recall pictures of gatherings at the Wailing Wall of Jerusalem, believed to be the Western Wall of the Second Temple. As written prayers are stuffed into the wall's crannies, murmurs rise from the gathered people. They raise their voices together, sometimes swaying back and forth, encouraging wholehearted participation in the practice, releasing personal inhibition and focusing together on a joint enterprise.

The Qur'an prescribes *salat*, or ritual prayer, for Muslims as one of the pillars of Islam. The prescription to pray five times each day comes from the *hadith*. The Qur'an itself spells out the need for ablution or purifying washing, praying in the direction of Mecca, appropriate dress, and the various postures of prayer. Sections of the Qur'an, particularly the first chapter, are among the prayers recited. The first chapter is recited during every *rakat*, or prayer cycle. Though *salat* can be solitary, the person practicing alone is aware of other Muslims praying simultaneously, since the prayers are offered at prescribed times. Often, the practice is carried out in a group—the power of numbers counts.

So does the beauty of the recitation. Though mosques may be decorated with stunning calligraphy of words from the scripture, the Qur'an is experienced primarily as oral, not simply read, but chanted, in particular musical intonations. There is even a name—*tilawat*—for the art of proper musical recitation of the Qur'an.

Even the most uttered Christian prayer—the Lord's Prayer, found in the gospel according to Matthew—is written in the nominative plural: "Give *us* this day *our* daily bread. Forgive *us* . . . as *we* forgive." Reciting the prayer together, as often happens in a variety of Sunday services and rites of passage, integrates scripture into practice. Similarly, the recitation of psalms, especially Psalm 23 ("The Lord is my shepherd . . ."), unites hearts and minds. The voices rising together in unison soften the singular number: The Lord is my shepherd, and yours and ours; we are joined together in praise.

Though the practice may seem rote to non-practitioners, those who recite prayers together find comfort and connection, unity and power, in the shared words. The scriptures and other utterances become more sacred as they are recited orally.

Chant

Chant is a specialized form of recitation. The practice of chant may be the earliest and most persistent form of religious practice. From Gregorian chant to Tuvan throat singing, from American Indian powwow music to ancient Vedic chant, from Jewish cantillation to Muslim *tilawat*, chant crops up across religious traditions, geography, and culture. Though sometimes elaborate, chant is distinguished from song by repetition and simplicity. On the other hand, chant's rhythm and tone distinguish it from simple recitation. So, chant is somewhere between recitation and song. One matches pitch and volume to others who are chanting to create the sensation of loss of self. What's more, chant may internalize a teaching in a way that simply reading it cannot accomplish.

Chant may focus on the meaning of the words that are said, but more on the sound of the words. Consider the most basic chant, *om*, from the Hindu tradition. Various Hindu scriptures, including the Upanishads and the Brahmanas, recommend chanting *om*, or *aum*, stressing the three different sounds that are pronounced, as a way of summing up all that is. The Taittirīya Upanishad even says "this whole world is *om*."[19] The single word is often chanted at the beginning and end of scriptural readings, is embraced by yoga practitioners, and serves as the most recognized symbol of Hinduism (ॐ).

Buddhism shares Hinduism's commitment to chant. Every form of Buddhism seems to have its own particular chant practice. From short *gathas* (verses in which the meanings matter more than the sounds) to *dharanis* (which express the essence of a teaching with sounds that affect the chanter's mind) to full sutras, the majority of Buddhist chant originates in scripture. Though individuals can chant alone, the primary practice is communal, as it is in Judaism and Islam, so that the chanter is immersed in and surrounded by the sound, breathing chant in as if it were air. Maezumi Roshi tells us:

> Chanting is an effective means of harmonizing body and mind. Chant with your ears, not with your mouth. When chanting, be aware of the others who are also chanting. Blend your voice with their voices. Make one voice, all together. Chant not too high, not too low, not too fast, not too slow. Take your pace from the senior practitioner, who will take the initiative. Chanting should not be shouting. When a person chants like that, he [*sic*] chants as if only he exists and no one else, which is not so. Always adjust yourself to the others, rather than expecting them to adjust to you. Then there is harmony. Chant as though each syllable were a drop of rain in a steady shower. It is very mild, consistent, and sustained.[20]

That advice is applicable whatever form of chant one practices. I have lost myself in chant at Taizé—an ecumenical

Christian community in France—chanting *Ubi Caritas*, a hymn whose verses Jacques Berthier took from 1 Corinthians 13. Similarly, neo-pagan chant has moved me into unity as names of the goddess—Isis, Astarte, Diana, Hecate, Demeter, Kali, Inana—have resounded in and through me.

Whichever text is used, the experience of chanting it allows the meaning to seep into the chanter. It creates a spiritual experience in that moment and encourages memorization without much effort. In Islam, this has been a primary focus of chant—to instill the words of the Qur'an into the believer. Then, chanters can revisit the words whenever they might need them for comfort, encouragement, or reframing of an experience. The words come alive in a way that isn't possible through simple reading.

This is why, for centuries, Christian monks and nuns have sung the Psalms, allowing the ancient prayers to live in them and through them, the singers always able to access their connection to God, regardless of the feelings they experience. This is also why Zen monks have chanted the sutras to live fully into the teachings of Buddha.

Lectio Divina

How does one read scripture as spiritual practice? It's nothing like the kind of analysis seen in the last two chapters. Instead, a spiritual reading lets go of interpretations, information, and ideas and asks instead straightforwardly, "What are these words saying to me today?" In looking at the ancient practice of *lectio divina*, we see that the idea of freedom of interpretation of the

Bible isn't a modern invention designed to make it more palatable to contemporary readers. We also learn a practice that explicitly seeks to connect the stories and prayers of an ancient people to the modern-day and specific concerns of any reader. It was described by the twelfth-century Carthusian monk Guigo II, but was practiced as early as the sixth century. The exercise consists of four parts: reading, meditation, prayer, and contemplation. The subtle differences among the four steps may confuse those of us outside monastic orders. First, the reader reads a short scripture at least twice, very slowly, often aloud, or with moving lips. The reader considers what the words say, the meaning of the passage, what happens in the text, and what the author is striving to communicate. While reading, a word or phrase may capture for the individual the meaning of the scripture at this particular time in this particular place. The identification of that word or phrase leads to the meditation stage, where the word(s) are considered along with the question, "How does this speak to my life?" The prayer stage comes as the meditator formulates a response to offer to God. Finally, in contemplation, the practitioner rests in the divine. Guigo summarizes it this way:

> Reading puts as it were whole food into your mouth; meditation chews it and breaks it down; prayer finds its savour; contemplation is the sweetness that so delights and strengthens. Reading is like the bark, the shell; meditation like the pith, the nut; prayer is in the desiring asking; and contemplation is in the delight of the great sweetness. Reading is the first ground that precedes and leads one into

meditation; meditation seeks busily, and also with deep thought digs and delves deeply to find that treasure; and because it cannot be attained by itself alone, then he sends us into prayer that is mighty and strong.[21]

Though a specifically Christian practice, *lectio divina* can be applied to any spiritual reading and invites an intuitive, rather than rational, awareness of a work. The identified word or phrase gives the reader an easy way to remember the passage and carry it into daily life. The unhurried practice encourages depth and deliberation, even leisure. Images and ideas arise spontaneously, making connections with daily life that would not come with a quick perusal or a more conventional form of study. The reader finds something in the scripture with personal meaning and application. Over time, these meanings, particularly the words and phrases that summarize the passage, come to be a collection of resources the reader can bring to mind when needing inspiration or encouragement.

In group practice, the passage is often read by two different voices, and the meditation, prayer, and contemplation happen individually, though the group may share insights afterward.

Lectio divina is not the only approach to spiritual reading and meditation. Variations have developed over the years in different traditions. Religious writer, translator, and professor Eknath Eswaran includes what he calls passage meditation as part of his recommended spiritual discipline, encouraging memorization of scripture. Using a memorized passage as a focus for meditation hones the mind and provides spiritual wisdom to rely on whenever needed.

Ignatian Contemplation

Ignatius Loyola, best known as the founder of the Jesuits, began his religious exploration as a wounded warrior, literally. Recovering from a serious injury in the Battle of Pamplona in 1521, he found himself with little to do but read the Bible and the lives of the saints, which prompted a religious conversion. Dedicating his life to God, he used his transcendent experiences while recovering to develop a set of prayer and meditation practices that draw from scripture. Known simply as the "Spiritual Exercises of Ignatius," they can be completed in either a thirty-day retreat or a longer "retreat in daily life," in which participants add a prayer regimen to their usual routines.

One particular exercise called "contemplation" involves reading biblical stories. The practice invites an imaginative exploration of a story. The reader moves into the narrative, using all the senses: hearing what is going on in the elements of the story and adding extras like street sounds or bird song, whatever comes to mind in reflection. The reader sees the people, the environment; notices details of clothing and objects; smells food or sweat or whatever comes up in the story; feels the air; and maybe even tastes food. The reader finds a role in the story and becomes one of the characters, either an individual from the written narrative, or an imaginary person—someone in a gathered crowd, for example—and experiences the story through that selected person. The contemplation includes the emotions that come up for the character through the story. The process is to fully experience the scene and all that happens in order to become intimate with the story.

Ignatius particularly encouraged use of contemplation with the gospels, but the technique can help enliven any story-based scripture. Using imagination as a tool may take away from the historical accuracy of the text but will move practitioners more deeply into their own interpretations and connect them with the text in a natural way so that it comes alive. The technique allows insights to emerge that relate to one's own life.

Divination with the I Ching

Some religions try to provide adherents with ways of accessing the unseen realm to help with decision-making in the material world. Many different techniques are used for divination. Best known may be the I Ching, one of the oldest written texts in the world, predating both Confucianism and Taoism, yet now sacred to both. It's even recognized as one of the Five Books of Confucianism.

In the traditional process of I Ching divination, the practitioner, after determining a question, uses a bunch of fifty yarrow sticks sorted into stacks in order to randomly generate a series of numbers, repeating the process three times. Later variations of the process used six tosses of three coins. Either system produces a six-layered hexagram of broken (*yin*) and unbroken (*yang*) lines. Each pattern of the sixty-four possible hexagrams represents particular changes in the universe and corresponds to a particular Chinese character, and a brief explanation of that character is given in the I Ching. The diviner, then, determines which hexagram the throw has revealed and reads the corresponding interpretation to derive the answer to the posed question.

This explanation, though, does not capture the richness of the I Ching. To begin to understand the role of such a book, we have to touch on the differences between Chinese and Western written language. Written language in the West is based on letters that correspond to particular sounds, the combination of which produces words as they are spoken. In contrast, Chinese written language consists of ideograms, symbols that represent physical objects, combined to form concepts or ideas. So reading Chinese is a profoundly different process than reading English or French, or even Russian or Arabic—one that is visual, instead of focused on sounds. While a process like *lectio divina* produces sound elements in which we immerse ourselves, the I Ching divination is directed more toward visual symbols that may be contemplated. At the same time, the process is firmly rooted in daily life, so the answers sought tend toward the practical rather than the philosophical.

Each of the I Ching's sixty-four hexagrams is composed of two trigrams, each of which has images (such as "mountain" and "lake"), qualities (such as "depth" or "satisfaction"), directions (such as "south"), time of year, and other attributes assigned to it. The combination of the trigrams results in the hexagram's interpretation as a concept such as "creative power," "resolution," "obstacles," or "community."

Selecting the question begins the process and prepares the mind for the ritual. Simple yes-or-no questions won't do. While the question should concern a specific situation or circumstance and be clear about time and people involved, it

should also be open-ended, seeking a way or striving to understand a status or determining potential effects of an action.
This way, the questioner's mind is opened to possibilities rather
than narrowed to specific options. The resulting hexagram,
ideogram, and interpretation work together with the questioner's state of mind to produce insights into the situation. The
process has psychological as well as spiritual elements.

Sitting in meditation with the images can bring new
insight. As in *lectio divina*, one can take a word or phrase that
jumps out in the interpretation, or even one of the simple
hexagrams, and contemplate it. If the mind wanders, we bring
it gently back to the image. In time, something may come to
the meditator in answer to the question asked.

It's not all in one's head, or only in the particulars of an
individual's life. I Ching specialists emphasize how the book
spells out the cosmic order. Translated as "Book of Changes,"
the text particularly relates to the movement and order of the
universe. The process of divination, then, places the individual in relation to the larger, universal system. As the Confucian commentary says of the I Ching:

> The Book of Changes contains a fourfold tao of the holy
> sages. In speaking, we should be guided by its judgments;
> in action, we should be guided by its changes; in making
> objects, we should be guided by its images; in seeking an
> oracle, we should be guided by its pronouncements.
>
> Therefore the superior man [sic], whenever he has to
> make or do something, consults the Changes, and he does
> so in words. It takes up his communications like an echo;
> neither far nor near, neither dark nor deep exist for it, and

thus he learns of the things of the future. If this book were not the most spiritual thing on earth, how could it do this? [1.10.1–2]

Chun Tzu, translated here as "superior man," is actually the virtuous or humane person, one who demonstrates *ren*, one who treats others as they would wish to be treated. If one is to be guided by Confucian ideals, engagement with the spiritual process of I Ching is fundamental.

Other traditions, including Islam and Christianity, have adopted divination as an approach to scripture, often simply opening a text at random to find answers to life questions. Though religious leaders often condemn this approach, the folk practice thrives.

Kabbalah

Celebrities and spiritual dabblers have popularized Kabbalah as an esoteric mystic practice. The teachings are ancient, though, rooted in traditional Jewish thought about the nature of scripture. As with Christian and Islamic practitioners, Jews understand biblical texts to have different levels of interpretation, from the most literal to the most symbolic. Specifically, Judaism defines four levels of interpretation: *peshat*, the plain meaning of the text; *remez*, the allegorical interpretation just below the surface meaning; *derash*, holding the portion of the text in comparison to other bits and building on the tradition, even creating *midrash*; and *sod*, the secret, hidden meaning, often revealed mystically. Together, interpretation using the four levels is called *pardes* (meaning orchard), combining the beginning letter of each level. The methods implied by these four terms have been debated throughout Jewish history, but we can describe them in general as follows: *Peshat* is not as simple as a literal rendering, but includes the traditional teaching about the text, as well as the literary and historical context. *Derash*, in contrast, may remove a text entirely from its specific situation. The practice of *midrash* that the rabbis engage in throughout the Mishnah and Talmud continually interweaves different passages to create elaborations of stories, plays on words, and unexpected juxtapositions of law and poetry, all of which become part of the tradition. *Ramez* provides a less elaborate, more straightforward symbolic system of allegory—for example, reading the two lovers in Song of Songs as God and Israel. The Song of Songs, sometimes called the Song of Solomon, tells a love story with the lovers themselves as its narrators. On the surface, a shepherd king seems to be in love with a beautiful woman. Never does the book make a comparison with God. Only interpreters have drawn that comparison, a strong example of *ramez*.

Jews consider all of these ways of working with texts as spiritual practice as well as study. Personal experience and perspective enter the process in *derash* and *sod* in particular. All require extensive familiarity with Tanakh and Talmud, and though intuitive connections are fine, it's not a casual or cavalier practice. In referring to *sod*, legend tells us that four prominent rabbis of the Mishnah period visited paradise (or *pardes*, the same word that is used for the layers of interpretation, in a play on words that is typical of Jewish interpretation). Of them, only Rabbi Akiba came and went in peace. The others died, lost their minds, or destroyed what was before them (that is, cut down the foundations of faith). Such stories warn scholars against the mystical exploration of Judaism without suitable training and personal faith. Some rabbis declare that only married men at least forty years old can study Kabbalah!

Kabbalah is a spiritual system of Jewish study that dwells in the mystical, or *sod*, level of scripture interpretation. In addition to the Hebrew Bible, the primary text is the Zohar (which means radiance or glow), a book that comments on mystical interpretation of the Torah along with other spiritual formulations and explorations. Some believe that the Zohar is part of the oral Torah, revealed to Moses, or perhaps even to Adam, but not written until the second century CE. Most modern scholars, however, date it to thirteenth-century Spain. The Zohar includes interpretations of the books of the Torah, accounts of famous rabbis discussing hidden traditions, secret prayer practices, explorations of the *mitzvot* (commandments), and commentaries on the afterlife.

The Zohar is far from the only source for Kabbalah. Esoteric Jewish practices appeared early in the Common Era, if not before, but most scholars believe that Kabbalah itself, like the Zohar, emerged in the Middle Ages. While all schools of Kabbalah endeavor to yield greater knowledge of and connection with God, various schools have distinct goals and doctrines. Jewish scholars describe two different forms of Kabbalah: practical and contemplative. Practical Kabbalah, or Kabbalah *Ma'asit*, entails achieving physical effects through metaphysical means, understanding the organization of the universe in order to manipulate it to one's ends—whether to cure an illness, perform divination through dreams, or, in the lore, to create a *golem* (a human-like creature). Contemplative Kabbalah, Kabbalah *Iyunit*, explores the nature of the divine through experience, a mystical striving. While Kabbalah *Ma'asit* veers into the magical and occult, contemplative Kabbalah is closer to the mainstream, claiming knowledge imparted by significant rabbis such as Nahmanides (also called Ramban) and his teacher, Isaac the Blind. Hasidic Judaism draws deeply from Kabbalah, particularly the interpretations of sixteenth-century Rabbi Isaac Luria. With some exceptions, the majority of kabbalistic texts and practices today are contemplative.

The mystical nature of Kabbalah forced it out of popularity during the Enlightenment. Although Hasidic Jewish communities would still draw lessons from its teachings, most scholars and rabbis dismissed it as "folk magic." Scholar Gershom Scholem resurrected kabbalistic practice and study through his research in the twentieth century. His books spread its popularity even beyond Judaism. As spirituality has become more popular in the United States, many have turned back to kabbalistic teachings as a source of inspiration.

Fundamental to Kabbalah's understanding of G-d (the name of the deity is never to be pronounced in Orthodox Judaism) is the separation of G-d from material reality. The universe, according to Kabbalists, is composed of *yesh*, which includes material things and concepts, anything with a beginning and an end, all that can be distinguished. *Yesh* is neutral, neither good nor bad, but is not all there is. Rather, *ayin*, or nothingness—or perhaps more accurately, "no-thingness"; that which has no boundaries or beginning or end—is that which is of G-d, and pervades the universe and infuses *yesh*. That which is without end (*ayn-sof*) is G-d, and Kabbalists strive to merge with it, to understand themselves as merged with G-d.[22]

Kabbalah envisions ten attributes or emanations, also called *sefirot* (meaning spheres) of G-d. They are often depicted as part of the Tree of Life or Tree of Knowledge, associated with the Garden of Eden. The *sefirot* include the divine feminine (*shekinah*) and correspond to ten levels of creation. Understanding the various connections requires years of study. Unpacking the *sefirot* is meant to lead to understanding the mind of G-d. Ethics also proceed from the emanations. Biblical passages that include mystic and symbolic correspondences, including Ezekiel's chariot prophecy, Isaiah's Temple vision, and Jacob's ladder, receive special attention from Kabbalists.

As in conventional Judaism, G-d needs humanity to complete *tikkun olam*—the repair of the world. One story tells that light emerged in creation and broke into bits accidentally. Human beings have the capacity to find these broken bits, these hidden lights, to make them visible, and to restore the wholeness. This repairing of the cosmos can even redeem evil. The way to *tikkun olam*, according to Kabbalah, happens through human performance of *mitzvot*: following with care and obedience the commands that G-d has given. What could look to an outsider like rote exercise—precision in following food laws, for example, or voicing the various blessings associated with daily routines—becomes a deeply spiritual endeavor of connecting with G-d to co-create and redeem the universe.

Non-Jews have discovered Kabbalah, so its influence has widened. Besides universalistic Jewish groups that teach Kabbalah, various secret societies and New Age teachers have adopted some of its traditions. All are rooted, though, in Jewish scripture, always beginning with the Torah.

What Do These Approaches Share?

Obviously, prayer, chant, *lectio divina,* Ignatian contemplation, I Ching divination, and Kabbalah study diverge widely from one another. They apply themselves to texts of different religions, and their practices rarely resemble one another. What they do share is a commitment to opening the mind and heart to listen to the texts in a creative way, letting go even of the words themselves if they get in the way, in order to find a deeper personal truth. Some might say the task is to connect with a larger spirit at work in the world. Others could see it as moving into the deepest Self. For those practices that are communal, there's a unity with others that's included. Whether we are reaching upward, inward, or across to one another, we're entering an intuitive, right-brain realm, the domain of dreams, intuition, and imagination. That means making connections that may sound like nonsense within a linear, logical approach, but who says knowledge must always be linear and logical? Certainly not the rabbis, as we'll see in the next interpretation, an example of how the rabbinic tradition works with scripture in an educated but open and insightful way, deepening into different levels of scriptural interpretation while attentive to intuitive jumps.

A Reading from Genesis Midrash Rabbah

R. Simon said: When the Holy One, blessed be He, came to create Adam, the ministering angels formed themselves into groups and parties, some of them saying, "Let him be created," whilst others urged, "Let him not be created." Thus it is written, *Love and Truth fought together, Righteousness and Peace combated each other* (Ps. LXXXV, 11): Love said, "Let him be created, because he will dispense acts of love"; Truth said, "Let him not be created, because he is compounded of falsehood"; Righteousness said, "Let him be created, because he will perform righteous deeds"; Peace said, "Let him not be created, because he is full of strife." What did the Lord do? He took Truth and cast it to the ground. Said the ministering angels before the Holy One, blessed be He, "Sovereign of the Universe! Why dost thou despise Thy seal! Let Truth arise from the earth!" Hence it is written, *Let truth spring up from the earth* (ib. 12). . . .

R. Huna the Elder of Sepphoris said: While the ministering angels were arguing with each other and disputing with each other, the Holy One, blessed be He, created him. Said He to them: "What can ye avail? Man has already been made!"[23]

Genesis Midrash Rabbah 8:5, translated under editors R. Dr. H. Freedman and Maurice Simon

97

GENESIS RABBAH interprets the book of Genesis through *midrash*, a rabbinic practice that builds on connections across various biblical texts, often adding in stories, myths, oral traditions, legal rulings, and even apparent inventions. Puns, word play, and definitional distinctions create and elaborate the connections between seemingly unconnected verses and ideas. This is not to say that the rabbis were completely inventing the complex interpretations. *Midrash* proceeds according to rules in an order recognized by the participants and the educated readers. The style has been described as "laconic, pithy, and terse, at times to the point of obscurity."[24] Yet, it's also playful and imaginative.

This particular book of *midrash* probably was produced shortly after the Jerusalem Talmud, around the fifth century, although it contains teachings of rabbis of previous centuries. Unlike other similar works, it offers a running commentary of about one hundred chapters, all related to the verses of the book of Genesis. While attending to the Torah text, the rabbis were also commenting on contemporary issues and Jewish traditions and laws, so sometimes the challenge of our modern understanding comes from lack of knowledge about the particular social and political context in which the rabbis found themselves.

Who are these rabbis? They are spokesmen of their time and to their culture. They have extensive knowledge of the Tanakh and of previous interpretations, including folklore and tradition. Esteemed in their community, they hold more than religious authority, for they are also the expositors of the law and tradition. They are links in a chain of tradition that their community saw as extending back to the giving of the Torah to Moses at Mount Sinai. Their preserved words carry weight.

The Rabbis' Commentary

This particular excerpt offers a story about the creation of Adam, the first human. Earlier in the text, the rabbis have discussed how Adam was originally created not as a man, but as an amalgam of man and woman, a figure similar to those of Plato's Symposium, who have to be split into their component genders. The rabbis base their image on the scripture "male and female he created them." (Genesis 1:27)

In this excerpt, the rabbis offer another story, this one about the angels arguing over the creation of human beings. And though they have previously acknowledged both male and female are created, they use "him" in reference to the human whose creation is the subject of dispute.

Nowhere in Genesis does it say that God created angels, but the rabbis are concerned about the verse (Genesis 1:26) that quotes God as saying, "Let *us* make man in our own image." The commentators justify the plural form in various ways. One suggestion is that God consulted with his ministering angels, the personified qualities of Love, Truth, Righteousness, and Peace, taken from a passage in the Psalms. With that suggestion, they're off on the story.

We don't know where these angels came from or what role they played in creation, but they seem to be giving God suggestions or guidance, which God completely ignores, going ahead and creating the human while the angels argue over whether or not it should be done.

As is typical in *midrash*, a verse from another part of the Bible is cross-referenced here. The commentators go to Psalms 85, explaining it as part of the angels' discourse. Not that love, truth, righteousness, and peace appear as angels in the psalm; rather, they are abstract qualities that God helps bring into being to offer salvation to his people. Yet, here in the interpretation of Genesis, the qualities are represented as different names for angels. Strangely, some translations of Psalms 85:11 differ quite a bit from this one, picturing Love, Truth, Righteousness, and Peace, not as competing and fighting, but as meeting and kissing! What on earth are we to make of all this?

The passage tells us a bit about the rabbis' view of humanity. In the back of their minds, they are working up to the idea that each creation has been named as "good," until we come to the creation of humans. Several verses in Genesis (1:26–30) relate specifically to the creation of humanity and God's speech to them. However, never does it include the formulaic "God saw that it was good" that occurs with each of the previous creations. In Genesis 1:31, however, God considers the whole of creation and calls it "very good." The rabbis expect that their readers know all this.

So, why was the creation of the human not called "good"? That is what the rabbis likely are trying to explain with this story about the angels' argument. At the moment of creation, no one knows whether humanity will be good. Humans will love, yet they will lie. They will do good deeds and create strife. The angels know this already, even though humanity has not yet been created. Somehow in *midrash*, all time is simultaneous; commentary on Abraham can come from the prophets, or vice versa, and insights into early psalms can come from much later texts. Anyway, the angels' argument addresses the nature of humanity. Can this creation be called good? Can humanity justify its existence?

God isn't too happy with this dispute among the spirits. He throws Truth, who is arguing against the creation of human beings, to the ground. Truth's cohorts object, quoting the psalm again, to invite Truth to spring up. And the angels continue their spat. Doesn't matter; while they fight, God goes ahead and makes Adam!

Another Take

Suppose that the angels had more influence. Truth and Peace insist that humanity will destroy them; Love and Righteousness object that goodness would prevail in humankind. The sides are drawn. The contest heats up. All these passions of God whirl together in anger, God set against Godself. When Truth is flung to the ground, does God repent? Perhaps Truth needs to be attended to. What will this creature, humanity, become? Is it worth making such a species? And then, the inspiration comes.

Humans, in the image of God, will find love at odds with truth. In striving for righteousness, people will disturb the peace. God will create humans in the image of God, male and female, loving and lying, good and disruptive, struggling internally and in their world to make the best of it they can.

Perhaps, then, in humanity, love can find a way to meet together with truth. Righteousness and peace may kiss one another.

Such is the playfulness with texts that the rabbis engage in, which could inspire us to do the same.

CHAPTER SIX

The Question of Translation

No one can understand the sounds of a drum
without understanding both drum and drummer;
nor the sounds of a conch without understanding
both the conch and its blower; nor the sounds
of a vina without understanding both vina and
musician.

> Brihadaranyaka Upanishad 2.4.7–2.4.9,
> translated by Eknath Easwaran

MORE THAN ONCE, people have asked me as a minister, "What translation of the Bible should I read?"

The simple answer is, "It depends."

The same question and answer apply to any other scripture.

As we've seen, each particular text is embedded in a unique time, place, and social location. Each has its own cultural context. One fragment of a cultural context is language. Few sacred texts were originally written in English, which means that contemporary American readers, if they are to appreciate a scripture, must shift their minds to a cultural context outside their own and either learn a new language or turn to translations. Few have the dedication to devote themselves to mastering a new language (myself included!), so finding reliable translations is a priority.

To figure out which translation is most appropriate, you have to consider your purpose when reading. If you're looking for the most technically accurate translation, you will want to make a different choice than if you're seeking spiritual guidance, ease of reading, or flowing words. You may want something that provides more interpretation or explanation to help you comprehend the text. Trying to grasp the tenor of the scripture's time and place may require a different rendition than getting an intuitive feel for the message. Always, though, the issue of trust in the translator comes up.

First, some other considerations.

Is Translation Even the Right Word?

Translation, transliteration, interpretation, adaptation—lots of words can be connected with a scriptural text. They are not equivalent.

Transliteration means changing a word from one writing system to another. Hebrew ‏חֶסֶד‎ becomes *hesed*, a word often translated as "loving-kindness" or "mercy," but those who know Hebrew contend it's difficult to fully capture the nuances of the word in English. Sometimes, then, it is simply rendered *hesed* in English translation.

Similarly, Chinese ideograms might be converted to English letters, such as using *li*, for the central Confucian theme of "the proper way," "ritual," or "custom." Hindu texts in English may retain terms like *brahman* and *atman* when they explain the relation of the essence or soul of the universe to individual souls. So, as ideas move from one language to another, essential terms may not be translated but transliterated, a clear demonstration of one challenge of translation.

A translation goes further than transliteration, as it renders one language into another language—rarely word for word, because skilled translators strive to bring the full meaning of the text to life in the second language. This is not an easy task. Linguist and humorist Richard Lederer recounts the awkward computer translation of a scriptural text, in which "The spirit is willing, but the flesh is weak" turned into "The wine is good, but the meat is spoiled."[25] The words were translated, but not their meaning.

Translation requires more than knowledge of vocabulary and grammar. Over and over, poets and critics have complained about how inadequate translation is in conveying the meaning and, especially, the beauty of an original text. As Robert Frost said, "Poetry is what gets lost in the translation." In the case of texts from a particular religious tradition, translators need to know the ancient languages, the culture in which they were embedded, and the evolution of the tradition.

Such challenges lead some traditions, notably Islam, to reject translations of their scripture. Because the Qur'an was originally received and written in Arabic, the only official Qur'an must be in Arabic. Altering the words would cause the essence of the scripture to be lost. Hence, according to Muslims, the Qur'an is never translated, but is "interpreted" in another language, or the *meaning* is said to be translated. Non-Muslims may call that a quibble, but the focus on the original language reminds us that any time we extend ourselves across culture and language, we enter a foreign domain that we are unlikely to fully understand.

Take, for example, the rendering of the ninety-nine names of God, which Islamic *hadith* describe as the list of the various ways God is referred to in the Qur'an—in Arabic, of course. All nouns carry gender in Arabic, so the list divides almost equally between feminine and masculine names, with fifty often identified as feminine. In translation, the gendered aspect of the names gets lost and Allah becomes, because of our own language-based assumptions, a more thoroughly masculine entity. In translation, we lose the nuanced associations.

Many other traditions, though, recognize translations of their scriptures as still conveying the same meaning. Translation means literally "to carry across" from one language and culture to another. So there are dozens of translations, often called versions, of the Christian and Hebrew Bible. Some denominations prefer particular versions.

We also find interpretations or adaptations of scriptures that are not direct translations but communicate the essence or meaning of a scripture in a more accessible way for the culture of the reader. An adaptation might rework prayers for modern situations or change the characters in a story to contemporary people. For example, the Good Samaritan might be depicted as an Arab or a transgender person. Interpretations might also elaborate on some of the historical and social context of a text. If a text is difficult or culturally remote, adaptations and interpretations help explain it. Sometimes, the best way to learn what a book is about is to find a children's version that explains it simply and clearly! On the other hand, it's important to keep in mind when using an adaptation or interpretation that it does not have the authority of a translation, because it has been reworked enough to be further distant from the original. Sometimes, adaptations or interpretations are created by people who can't even read the original language of the text!

Questions About Translations

No particular translation will be right for all readers. Consider your own priorities, as well as what the translation provides. Are you seeking a text that is historically and culturally accurate? One with language that is vivid and exciting? That provides additional explanations of challenging concepts? Your personal aims should be most influential in deciding which translation to choose.

You could select a translation that is commonly used, though that may not be your best choice. A quick online search may give a clear answer; on the other hand, the Internet may rely more on public domain texts that are older and may be less authoritative. The most used translation may not match your own goals.

For example, with more than forty different versions of the Bible, your choices can be overwhelming. The New International Version of the Bible may be the most read today—it's certainly the biggest seller—but probably has a more evangelical bent than most Unitarian Universalists would be comfortable with. We might prefer the New Revised Standard

Version because of its widespread use in academic settings and its commitment to gender-neutral language. Adapted from the Revised Standard Version, first published in the middle of the twentieth century, it's a product of a team of scholars, as so many of the biblical translations are. The King James Version is prized for the poetry of its language, but, of course, misses out on up-to-date scholarship and, being removed from today by several centuries, uses forms of English long ago abandoned. There is a New King James Version that updates the language and scholarship while retaining the style of the original. The New American Bible and the New Jerusalem Bible are most commonly used among Catholics, while the Jewish Publication Society produces the most authoritative translation of the Hebrew Scriptures for Jews.

Some translations strive for formal equivalence, a word-for-word rendering, while others seek dynamic or functional equivalence, working to make the overall meaning clear and adjusting more for cultural and linguistic differences.

Some renditions of texts are actually adaptations—*not* translations at all—as with Eugene Peterson's popular *The Message* version of the Bible, or many of Stephen Mitchell's adaptations of texts such as Tao Te Ching or Bhagavad-Gita. Poets and writers like Peterson and Mitchell may produce the most readable or aesthetically pleasing works, but these are works written for contemporary Western readers and only loosely convey the meaning of the original text. When reading an adaptation like that, you are seeing the book through the adapter's eyes. Again, what you choose to read depends on *your* goals in reading.

Other questions you might consider about translation:

- Is the translator an individual or a team? Teams often have a broader perspective because they include various points of view and are more likely to catch errors and find ways to render ambiguous or challenging concepts. Yet, an individual may have a winning writing style.
- What is the translator's cultural and religious background? Are they associated with a particular sect or tradition within the religion, or are they from outside the religion entirely? How knowledgeable of English are they, and how did they come to learn English? A translator from Australia may have a different perspective on Asian religions than one from Scotland. A translator who comes from a tradition different from the one they are translating may have another valuable set of insights. For example, when the translators of the New Revised Standard Bible wanted to address problems of anti-Semitism that came from previous translations, they added a translator of Jewish background, even though their purpose was to translate for Christians.[26] An outside perspective helped produce a more holistic translation.
- What is the translator's academic background? Do they have a thorough knowledge of both (or all) the languages with which they are working? How did they come to know what they know? Are they professors of religion? Or of language? Or followers of the religion? Are they also poets or novelists, revealing a different kind of connection with language and comfort working with words? Any of these backgrounds, and others, might validate someone's work in

translation, but a poet and a religion professor are bound to approach a text with different priorities. Find a translator whose goals match your own.

• Is the translation associated with a particular group within a religion? For example, the New Jerusalem Bible is generally read by Catholics. That doesn't mean only Catholics should read it, but we should recognize that it may read differently than a Bible usually read by and produced for evangelicals or mainline Protestants.

Detective Work

How can you find out the answers to the questions posed? First, ask people you trust. If you know someone who practices a religion that values a particular text, ask them what translation they use and what they like about it. Better yet, ask several people and compare their preferences. You may learn as much about the differences within religions as you do about the commonalities!

Then, read the preface, introduction, and notes or other accompanying information in the translation. Often, translators reveal something of their backgrounds and orientations directly. Sometimes, they'll talk about their influences and goals. Or, you may be able to read between the lines by considering, for example, whom they thank or acknowledge.

If there's limited information in the volume itself, begin your investigation online. Though online information can be mixed in terms of accuracy, you will find out if there is controversy, and also who is using the translation.

Comparing Translations

The late poet Maya Angelou said, "I read the Bible to myself; I'll take any translation, any edition, and read it aloud, just to hear the language, hear the rhythm, and remind myself how beautiful English is." Sometimes, any translation will do.

Other times, you want something specific.

I own several versions of the Bible and at least a couple translations of the Bhagavad-Gita, Qur'an, Gnostic scriptures, and Tao Te Ching. I supplement those with online and library texts. Different translations awaken different ideas and emotions for me. If I want a story, I may use *The Message* Bible, while I read Psalms from the King James Version for their beauty, and delve into the New Revised Standard for an authoritative look at Paul's letters. With the Tao Te Ching, I'll read Stephen Mitchell for the beauty and accessibility, but Gia-Fu Feng and Jane English for more accurate translation, the inclusion of the Chinese characters, and the accompanying photos.

Reading different translations side by side can bring a deeper understanding of the subtleties of the text. While we may never fully understand a language we do not speak and read ourselves, seeing different translators' versions opens up possibilities and complexities, shades and shadows, that might otherwise prove elusive. That's what we'll do with I Ching 17.

A Reading of I Ching 17

Hexagram 17 of the I Ching

Translation One

Adapting brings exceptional progress. There is an advantage in correct persistence. Then there will be no mistake.

Growth (thunder) in the midst of excess (lake) forms the condition for Adapting. An enlightened person, therefore, when in darkness, leads the way within for a comforting rest.

The Illustrated I Ching,
translated by R. L. Wing

Translation Two

FOLLOWING has supreme success.
Perseverance furthers. No blame.
Thunder in the middle of the lake:
The image of FOLLOWING.
Thus the superior man at nightfall
Goes indoors for rest and recuperation.

I Ching: Or, Book of Changes,
translated by Richard Wilhelm
and Cary F. Baynes

THE I CHING has served as a divination tool for thousands of years. No one knows exactly its origins, though legends point to antiquity. Its text describes how to interpret the particular set of lines generated by throwing straws or coins to produce a code of short and long lines, based on the combinations that come from multiple tosses. Each series of tosses results in a six-line symbol, called a hexagram. The hexagram for I Ching 17 is shown above. Hexagrams are read from bottom to top in trigrams; the two trigrams here show two yin (broken) lines above one yang (unbroken), and one yin line above two yang lines. Together, they depict two symbols relating to one another—lake above thunder.

The brevity of the related Chinese text that interprets the hexagram makes it relatively easy to compare different translations. Subtle differences in wording can lead to divergent interpretations.

The two translations above each include two parts that come from different time periods: the first, known as the Judgment, and the second, the Image. The Judgment dates from at least 1000 BCE during the Zhou era. The Image interprets the hexagram and is often said to come from Confucius, though it's likely that it pre-dated him.

The translators provide additional commentary in their works, which I have omitted for the purpose of simplicity. Each commentary has its own form. Wilhelm and Baynes interpret the Judgment and the Image separately and then add an interpretation of the lines, so though their translation is shorter, their interpretation expands it. Wing interprets the Image and Judgment together, includes the Chinese characters, and puts

in related illustrations. She also appends the line-by-line interpretation at the end of her book.

What does this particular text address? The transliterated
title, *sui*, is translated by Wing as "adapting" and by Wilhelm
and Baynes as "following." The latter term here does not mean
letting go of one's own will. In fact, "following" includes leading, as a leader must listen and adapt to followers, and vice
versa. In short, all need to be in harmony, rather than striking
out alone. Each person adjusts to the environment. Wing recommends flexibility, and Wilhelm and Baynes remind us that a
leader "must first learn to serve." Whatever label is used for this
quality, these translators agree it leads to progress or success.

The next line, though translated differently, seems to agree
more closely in meaning. "There is an advantage in correct
adherence." "Perseverance furthers." Each sentence describes a
condition of holding firm. The final sentence is also similar:
"Then there will be no mistake." "No blame." Each sentence
clears the slate, finding nothing wrong, though our translators
use different words.

The Image sections more directly relate to the hexagram,
based on traditional associations of symbols with the hexagram.
Both translations name the thunder appearing in relation to
the lake. They remind us to consider the circumstances as we
go through life. Both describe the person of wisdom going
inside to rest when night comes. Wing also tells of other qualities that the lake and thunder relate to (excess and growth).
The associations may be culturally specific, but sitting with
these images and connections in meditation, as described in
chapter 5, could be a productive endeavor.

Wilhelm and Baynes translate simply, with as few words as possible. The terseness, particularly in the Judgment, provides clear, if abstract, images to meditate on. This translation, though, does little to help us understand how the Image connects to the concept. What does thunder above a lake have to do with following?

Wing's use of the term "adaptation" rather than "following" helps me understand. If there is thunder around a lake, then one must, indeed, adapt. Having been out in the open when I've heard thunder, I know the need to change plans, to accommodate with the circumstances that exist. Thinking of that experience inspires me to value and appreciate adaptation, which could be seen as a form of following. Responding to conditions, I am alert to their direction and, as in a dance, follow them.

Also, it's helpful to understand the associations with thunder (growth) and lake (excess). Chinese ideograms through the centuries have acquired an elaborate system of connotations that speak on an unconscious as well as conscious level to people who know the written language. Identifying one of those connections for each image encourages me to dig more deeply into my own ideas about those images and see what may come up for me. Growth would not be a natural connection for me with thunder, nor would a lake with excess. Yet, a lake contains excess water, creating an expanse. Cities store their water supplies—the excess beyond what is used right now—in lakes. Lakes connote a vision of plenty: plenty of water that can then yield plenty of crops.

The resonance between thunder and growth is harder for me to find. In consulting various commentaries, I find that 17 is often associated with the seasons of life and of the year. Thunder in particular relates to spring, early morning, and the eldest son. The qualities of thunder include excitement and activity as well as growth. Reflecting, I do associate thunder with spring, though more often afternoon than early morning in my part of the world. There is a literal charge to the air as thunder appears, which is exciting, but threatening. To me the communication is, "Wake up. Be careful."

Each translator offers something to chew on. The differences remind me that different languages develop shades of meaning that are hard to convey to someone unfamiliar with that language. It's like looking at clues to meaning and gradually homing in on the depth of the images. Precision in both the denotations and connotations of communication is hard to attain. The reward comes when insights develop from considering the ways the translations agree and how their differences cast shadows that suggest coherence.

Confronting differences in translation can, itself, be a spiritual practice—listening for the personal resonances, exploring the images, immersing in the various aspects that appear by looking at the text through different lenses. Such exploration can produce fresh, unexpected insights.

PART II

A Unitarian Universalist Take on Scripture

CHAPTER SEVEN

How Unitarian Universalists Perceive Scripture

What is enshrined I do not know,
But the awe of a sense of gratitude
Brings tears to my eyes.

Saigyō Hōshi (Shinto)

HAVING EXAMINED the origins and interpretations of scripture, we've seen a range of approaches and ideas about it. Differences exist both within religious traditions and between them. How, then, do Unitarian Universalists view scripture? How do we responsibly read and use it, individually and within our congregations?

Many early Unitarians and Universalists in the United States came to their convictions by drawing on biblical texts. For example, in the late eighteenth century, Unitarian Joseph Priestley argued, "The Scriptures teach us that there is but one God, who is himself the maker and the governor of all things. . . . Not only does the word trinity never appear in the scriptures but it is no where said that there are three persons in this God."[27] He went on to cite a wide variety of scripture verses to document his case. Similarly, Universalist Hosea Ballou, in writing his famous *Treatise on Atonement*, stated his purpose as "to free the scripture doctrine of atonement from those encumbrances which have done it so much injury."[28]

So both Unitarians and Universalists in their early days in America grounded their theology in the biblical narrative. In fact, as they organized themselves, they asserted their reliance on scripture. William Ellery Channing's famous sermon, "Unitarian Christianity," which explained the thoughts of liberals in 1819, was grounded in I Thessalonians 5:21 ("prove all things; hold fast that which is good"). The Universalists in 1803 issued a profession of faith that said, "We believe that the Holy Scripture of the Old and New Testament contain a revelation of the character of God, and of the duty, interest and final destination of mankind [sic]." Notably, both left room for maneuvering, Channing by quoting a scripture that seemed to say one did not need to hold fast to all scripture, only "that which is good," leaving open the possibility for later setting aside of scriptural authority. Meanwhile the Universalists did not assert, even in 1803, that the Bible contained *the* revelation, but rather *a* revelation. That left open a door for other revelations.

It was easy to go too far, though. In 1824, Universalist minister Abner Kneeland was forced out of the ministry for rejecting the idea that the Bible was divinely inspired. Several years later he was convicted of blasphemy, and many Unitarian Transcendentalists joined in the petition for his pardon, though his prosecutor, too, was a Unitarian.

That single incident gives a sense of the variety of thought that existed within both denominations about the Bible and how to read it. The Transcendentalists, perhaps the most radical of Unitarians, found inspiration in German romanticism and in the historical-critical methods of biblical scholarship that were already arising in Germany. They embraced nature, intuition, and scripture from other traditions as equally important as the Bible. Most importantly, Transcendentalists reclaimed the personal experience of the transcendent. But not everyone agreed with them.

Though many Transcendentalists actually left Unitarianism, finding it too conservative, many members of the next generation of Unitarian ministers were swayed by the Transcendentalists. In 1867, the formation of the Free Religious Association brought together an assortment of religious leaders, including Unitarians and Universalists. In the effort to oppose dogmatism, they moved away from Christianity, seeing the Bible as a less significant source. The Western Unitarian Conference, organized in 1852, also took a more liberal stance toward Christianity, proclaiming in 1866, "We honor the Bible and all inspiring scripture, old and new," deliberately equating the Bible with other books. The 1893 Parliament of World's Religions introduced many Unitarians to other religious viewpoints and books, and provided an opportunity for some of the Parliament's speakers, like the Bengali Swami Vivekananda, to tour and explain their religious sources to Unitarian audiences.

Nevertheless, as in other Protestant churches, scripture reading held center stage in worship for most Unitarians and Universalists through the nineteenth century. As late as 1900, Universalist evangelist Quillen Shinn asserted, "Most heartily we believe in the Bible, and we stand for the spiritual interpretation of the sacred volume."[29] Even Universalists, though, had mixed opinions. While some stood fast on the authority of the Bible, others, particularly those influenced by Spiritualism—the huge movement in the latter part of the nineteenth century that sought communion with the dead— found their faith in biblical authority waning.

The loosening of the ties to Christianity opened the door to humanism within both traditions, especially among Unitarians, where John Dietrich and Curtis W. Reese expounded its tenets in the early twentieth century. Humanism's focus on people over deities moved Unitarians further from their scriptural roots. The *Humanist Manifesto* in 1933, signed by many Unitarians, one Universalist, and others, does not even mention scripture and asserts that "religious institutions, their ritualistic forms, ecclesiastic methods, and communal activities must be reconstituted as rapidly as experience allows." Humanists began purging their services of scriptural readings. And with the growth of the fellowship movement after World War II, humanism became more and more prevalent among Unitarians.

Meanwhile, some Universalists, stirred by leaders like Clarence Skinner and Clinton Lee Scott, started redefining their own movement, moving from the doctrine of universal salvation to an embrace of universal religion. Most, though, clung to the Universalist Christianity they knew best.

As these changes in thinking progressed, reliance on scriptural texts became less frequent. Still, the 1957 hymnal *Hymns of the Spirit*, developed for both Unitarian and Universalist churches, included sixteen orders of service, almost all of them including sentences taken from the Bible as opening words and with places to include "lessons," presumably from the Bible. By the time *Hymns for the Celebration of Life* was published in 1964, the previous format had disappeared and the biblical readings that remained mingled with many other source materials.

As the twentieth century widened our theological inclusiveness to fully accept humanism and, later, paganism, Bible readings became less and less common in worship. Other texts took the place of what we had conceived as scripture. Some churches, though, held onto their traditional scripture readings even into the twenty-first century, proving once more our theological diversity.

Without a Canon

In lists of scriptures from various traditions, the Unitarian Universalist faith never appears. We have no canon. When I was invited to read the scripture to represent Unitarian Universalism at my Harvard Divinity School graduation service, I had to think hard about my selection. Christians of various sorts were already doing biblical readings. A Buddhist had selected something from Buddhist texts. I needed to come up with something that was distinctly *ours*. I ended up drawing from Emerson's *Divinity School Address*. Though not set aside and labeled as canonical, that text as much as any seemed to reflect our unique religious stance, and was doubly appropriate since these were words Emerson had spoken to a graduating class more than a century-and-a-half earlier.

We Unitarian Universalists have not set apart particular works as our "scripture." Sure, we have hymnals and meditation manuals that designate specific readings as texts we draw from, but we are neither defined nor limited by those choices. Sacredness is often a core element of something being identified as scripture, but we tend to defy the division of the world into sacred and secular. If we don't set aside anything in particular as sacred, how can we even begin to approach scripture?

Without a canon, we could simply define scripture as any text that *any* religious group has stamped as sacred. The real test of something's merit as scripture is how it comes to be used by a religious group. Does the text inspire? Does it define a group in some way? Do group members treat it with authority? Do they use it in liturgy? Do they turn to it for guidance in life? Further, if we truly believe revelation never stops, we cannot close a canon.

But what does that have to do with us? For Unitarian Universalists, this happens at the level of individual congregations rather than at the denominational level. With no texts designated as sacred in any official way—or with all texts sacred—we have a great library from which to draw. We read the words of Martin Luther King Jr. with the same reverence that we accord to books labeled holy by others.

This approach creates a very open-ended definition of scripture. We recognize that the various techniques for understanding and using scripture, whether canonical or not, can be applied to other works, too. Unitarian Universalism posits an expansive approach. In our search for wisdom and inspiration, we don't like to stop at what has been designated as canonical hundreds of thousands of years ago. While not every text that has had meaning for an individual merits the distinction of being called scripture, we treat some texts as more profound, more uniting, more sacred than others, and we draw from them more often for individual and collective revelation. We can argue about which texts those might be, but we are unlikely ever to nail down a canon, as it is contrary to our openness to knowledge and understanding from whatever source is available. With whichever texts we might suggest as scriptural, however, we can use the same techniques of study and interpretation that have been applied to traditional scriptures.

Questioning and Embracing Scripture

Unitarian Universalists often come to our faith from other traditions, primarily Christian, many as I did, by finding flaws in the scriptural texts. Some have suffered scripture being used against them. People who are queer have been assaulted by quotations from Leviticus, condemning men who lay with other men to be stoned (though, it should be noted, women who lay with other women don't get a mention in Leviticus!). Women heard that they had no right to speak in church because Paul forbade it in the first century. With such experiences, no wonder Unitarian Universalists bristle at claims of scriptural authority.

Even Unitarian Universalists who don't feel personally attacked often question the scriptures with which they grew up. Stories of supernatural miracles strike us as they did Emerson in the nineteenth century, when he labeled Jesus' so-called miracles as monsters. Then there are the contradictions! How many animals did Noah take? Only two pairs of each, or seven pairs of some? It depends on whether you're reading Genesis 6 or 7. Did Moses receive the law at Mount Sinai or Mount Horeb? Exodus, Leviticus, and Nehemiah say the former; 1 Kings, 2 Chronicles, and Malachi, the latter. Did Jesus preach his most famous sermon on a mountain or in a field? Matthew says mountain, Luke says field—and the sermons are not the same! Many of us reason that if the Bible can't consistently and accurately report simple facts, how can we believe any of it? We Unitarian Universalists have balked at inconsistencies, cringed at stories of miracles, winced at indoctrination that placed men above women, and shaken our heads at precepts that defy reason.

On the other hand, we've seen already that these inconsistencies come about because the texts come from various sources. Recognizing these problems can encourage us to ask questions about them, rather than simply reject the texts as useless. And differences of detail may not disprove the spiritual truths the texts contain.

Having discovered the limitations of childhood teachings, though, many Unitarian Universalists have dipped their toes into other scriptural sources. Rejecting the Christian Bible, they sought spiritual wisdom elsewhere. They may have discovered Bahá'u'lláh or Rumi or the Dalai Lama, which then inspired digging into texts of Baha'i, Sufism, or Buddhism. They may have even converted and embraced another religious tradition. Enthusiasm may have been ignited or dissipated. Translating from other cultural contexts may have created frustration or intrigue—or both!

Some Unitarian Universalists who were raised in non-Christian religious traditions have struggled with their own scriptures as well, whether Jewish or Muslim or Hindu.

Unitarian Universalists may have read extensively in various texts—those they grew up with as well as others—but may not have found personal spiritual meaning in them. Still others have never had much exposure at all to scripture. When they do open a book of it, they find it confusing and inaccessible, wondering how it could possibly have earned the respect and adulation it has among religious adherents. Perplexed, they close the book, relieved they don't have to decipher it to save their souls. Still, they wonder if there might be something there.

On the other hand, many Unitarian Universalists continue to find succor in familiar passages they learned in childhood or that they studied as adults: "Consider the lilies of the field. They neither toil nor spin." "What does the Lord require of you but to do justice, love, mercy and walk humbly with your God?" "He has sent me to bring good news to the oppressed, to bind up the broken hearted, to proclaim liberty to the captives, and release to the prisoners . . ." There are Unitarian Universalists who chant the Heart Sutra of Buddhism, who meditate on Rumi's Sufi poetry, and who re-read the Bhagavad-Gita regularly.

Sometimes they stumble on deep meaning in texts not regarded as scripture in any traditional sense, but that have many of the qualities and even uses of scriptures. Not everyone would call them scripture, but many Unitarian Universalists have their favorites. Humanist Unitarian Universalist minister David Bumbaugh, for example, privileges the works of Ralph

Waldo Emerson, Theodore Parker, Henry David Thoreau, Kenneth Patton, Henry Nelson Wieman, and the *Humanist Manifesto*.[30]

As stated before, our religious tradition clearly draws from various scriptural traditions. Our original Unitarian Universalist Principles, drawn up in 1959 when the Unitarians and Universalists were working toward consolidation, needed a rewrite more than twenty years later, especially because they were not feminist-friendly. A committee developed a new set during the 1980s, received input from across the Unitarian Universalist Association (UUA), and determined the need to list sources of our tradition along with the Principles. The inspiration of "Jewish and Christian teachings" still spoke to many Unitarian Universalists, though there was disagreement about exactly how to state their degree of influence. That was one reason the Sources ended up separated out from the Principles. Also included in the 1985 version of the Sources was "Wisdom from the world's religions"—which also turns us toward scriptures. In fact, our 1993 hymnal *Singing the Living Tradition* includes readings from Buddhist, Sikh, Taoist, Confucian, Muslim, Hindu, Native American, Jewish, and Christian texts. Some of these readings are from the scriptures of those traditions, like the Dhammapada, the Bhagavad-Gita, and the Bible. Others are from prominent leaders in those traditions like Howard Thurman, Chaim Stern, Rabindranath Tagore, and Black Elk. Even some Unitarian Universalist authors have crept into the section labeled "Jewish and Christian Teachings."

In addition to world religions and Jewish and Christian teachings, though, we list four other sources. All of them have readings represented in the hymnal, too—from Unitarian Universalist authors, from various scriptures, and from religious and secular sources that range widely. One conclusion about a Unitarian Universalist approach to scripture is that we treat our many sources of inspiration as more or less equal. Words from the Bible and the Dhammapada are not held to be more compelling than words from Tagore or Black Elk. Or even words of poetry. As Unitarian Universalist minister Laurel Hallman has said:

> I believe that poetry is scripture. I believe that scripture is poetry. I believe that poetry is the way deep truth is transmitted from person to person and generation to generation. I believe that when Emily Dickinson said "Tell the truth/but tell it slant" she was speaking of metaphorical truth, the poetic truth that nourishes the heart, and opens the mind and communicates to the depths.[31]

Responsible Use of Scripture

Using these holy texts responsibly is a challenge. A Taoist story tells of students who burned Buddhist texts for warmth.[32] One of the students refused to burn the books, and then dreamed of the group of students being called before a tribunal, where his comrades were condemned to death. He learned to protect Buddhist texts, even though they were not his own tradition.

Symbols matter. We recognize that burning the Qur'an is a more serious act than burning a novel or book of poetry, even if we might personally regard the novel or poetry as being as scripturally authoritative as the Qur'an. The difference is in the attitudes and beliefs that Muslims hold about the book, and the respect we want to offer to Muslim people who embrace those beliefs. By showing respect for what any group deems sacred, we accept that community's beliefs, as different as they may be from our own.

While Unitarian Universalists might never be guilty of burning scriptures, even for warmth or political protest, misuse can take more subtle forms. At the same time, we reserve the right to argue with any text. Maintaining that delicate balance requires more than good intention. It requires understanding others' interpretations and feelings about their scriptures. To respectfully and honestly dispute—or endorse—ideas found in a text, we have to know all we can about the context of those texts and the way they have been understood by others over time and across cultures. This is a demanding, though extremely rewarding, discipline. We need to engage with the people for whom the texts have authority, as well as look at what the words say, both at face value and in their historic and cultural context.

At the same time, if we are to fully pursue our own spiritual journeys, we need to consider what texts have authority for us, individually and personally, as well as within our particular congregations and our broader movement. We need to dip deeply enough into scripture to determine what brings us inspiration and sets our own ethical norms and philosophical beliefs. Though we respect others' interpretations as we respect their opinions, we do not defer to them simply because they are religious ideals, but we do strive to engage with them.

Working Toward Pluralism

People's reactions to faiths different from their own vary along a wide spectrum. Harvard professor and world religions expert Diana Eck lists three basic attitudes: exclusion, assimilation, and pluralism.[33] Exclusionists fear that their own religion will be squeezed out if others are accepted as legitimate. They fight against the very presence of difference. Unitarian Universalists eschew exclusion of this kind as it violates our Principles of acceptance of one another and free and responsible search for truth, wherever that might lead. We appreciate and honor differences rather than seek to exclude because of disagreements.

People who favor assimilation tend to see their own religion as including and welcoming the other. Assimilationists, though, may see outward signs of another religion as threatening, arguing that Muslim women should not wear the veil or Christians should resist decorating with crosses, so that they don't remind us of our religious differences. Sometimes Unitarian Universalists can be guilty of embracing assimilation in an awkward way. For example, they may see the parallels between Unitarian Universalism and Baha'i or Sufi faiths as so clear that they suggest these other religions should simply join Unitarian Universalism, not understanding that this may be an affront to those who fully embrace their own distinctive tradition. Assimilationists may water down other traditions' scriptures and ideas in ways that make them more palatable to themselves. They may strive to find agreement where it doesn't really exist. This can result in reading scriptural texts in misleading ways.

Finally, pluralism, the ideal that Eck works toward, acknowledges real differences and lets them stand side by side. Pluralism invites dialogue and understanding of the distinctions between others and ourselves. Pluralism is entirely consistent with Unitarian Universalism. Not only do we strive to approach the religious world with a pluralistic attitude, we also have enough religious diversity within our ranks that even inside our congregations, a pluralist attitude is required.

Most of this chapter examines a Unitarian Universalist approach to what other groups have designated as their scriptures. Is there any scripture, then, that we can claim as a religious group? Sometimes when individuals find deep meaning in particular texts, their love of those passages grows so that their congregations, or even great numbers of Unitarian Universalists—perhaps even a majority—come to value them.

As already noted, no authority has set out a Unitarian Universalist canon. Any attempt would meet with arguments from all quarters. However, a few readings stand out. If you say the words, "Love is the spirit of this church," many Unitarian Universalists can complete the congregational covenant from memory, though each may quote the variation used in their own particular congregation. One of the most beloved and quoted texts in Unitarian Universalism serves as our next reading.

A Reading of "For So the Children Come"

For so the children come
And so they have been coming.
Always in the same way they come
   born of the seed of man and woman.
No angels herald their beginnings.
No prophets predict their future courses.
No wisemen see a star to show where to find the
babe that will save humankind.
Yet each night a child is born is a holy night,
Fathers and mothers—
sitting beside their children's cribs
feel glory in the sight of a new life beginning.
They ask, "Where and how will this new life end?
Or will it ever end?"
Each night a child is born is a holy night—
A time for singing,
A time for wondering,
A time for worshipping.

Sophia Lyon Fahs

THIS POEM first appeared in *Worshipping Together with Questioning Minds* in 1965, Fahs's book about leading children in worship.[34] By then, she had been writing and editing curricula for Unitarians for more than two decades. No one shaped Unitarian religious education for children in the twentieth century more than she did.

Since then, her words have been enshrined by Unitarian Universalists. Not only do they appear in our hymnal, but they have also been quoted in sermons, studied in curricula for adults and children, set to music, inscribed on walls, and used in ritual. The text is read on at least one of two particular ritual occasions in a large number of UU congregations: at child dedications and at Christmas celebrations. In both instances, Fahs's words amplify the particular Unitarian Universalist theological grounding of the occasion.

Fahs, as a mother of five children, knew whereof she spoke. Having watched two of her own children die and the other three grow into adults, she appreciated the wonder that is brought into the world each time a child is born. In the poem, she captures the combination of ordinariness and specialness that comes with every birth. One of the most common events people identify as sacred is the birth of their children, and that attitude pervades the poem. The words become a commentary on our UU acceptance of every person as they are, born into a holy moment. We are reminded of our embodied forms and of the role of sexuality in producing children ("born of the seed of man and woman"). And, as one might expect from Fahs, the questions parents ask in the poem lead to a sense of wonder.

Fahs makes no explicit mention of Jesus or Christmas, yet the reading may be the most commonly read at Christmas in Unitarian Universalist congregations. The words become a Christmas reading because her litany lists elements from the

story of Jesus' birth as told in Matthew and Luke. In contrast
to his story, however, regular births bring no angels, no wise
men, no stars in the East, no prophetic proclamations. Unitarian Universalists have long rejected the miraculous from the
Christmas story, while striving to hold onto the holy in it. Fahs
strikes the balance for us. Stripping the birth story of its apparent miracles, we are left with the birth. Every child, the poem
implies, is like Jesus, full of divine potential. So, in our UU
Christmas rituals, we don't welcome a king or lord, but a
human child. We reflect on our theological understanding of
the role of Jesus as fully human while we affirm the miraculous
mystery of birth, without supernatural heralds or symbols.

We know how Jesus' story comes out. Yet, at the moment of
birth, we don't know what will happen. Will the life end in
martyrdom? Will it end too early, as Fahs knew from her own
experience could happen? Will it end in fulfillment, producing
love and justice? Will this new life ever end? It seems incon-
ceivable as we wonder at cribside.

So, the poem becomes appropriate for a remembrance of
Jesus' birth and as a commentary on every birth. That makes it
appropriate for reading at a child dedication, a ritual commitment of a family and a congregation to a child's support and
development. Together, we rejoice in worship at a child added
to the community and welcomed into a family.

Reading these words on ritual occasions deepens their
meaning. In a congregation where the words are read at child
dedications, parents of other children hear them and remember their own commitments to the children they had dedicated
in the church. Children hear them and know they are among
those children who have come and been wondered at. Young

adults look forward to hearing the words said over their future children.

Fahs's reading has power for us because it articulates and embraces our theological understandings: that holiness is not contingent on veering outside the natural world, that Jesus represents the potential of all human children for sacred connection, and that we are united in our experience of birth, both as children and as parents. Recently, some have critiqued the poem as reinforcing heteronormative expectations because of the gendered references to "man and woman" and "fathers and mothers." We now understand that families have more diversity, and might edit the reading to be more universal. Nevertheless, the power of the reading multiplies as it is read at ritual occasions, and it has become a touchstone text for many individual Unitarian Universalists and congregations.

CHAPTER EIGHT

Preconceptions and Cultural Bias

My words are very easy to understand,
Very easy to practice.
No one under heaven can understand them,
No one can practice them.

Tao Te Ching 70,
translated by Stephen Addiss
and Stanley Lombardo

TRANSLATION, covered in chapter 6, is only one of the difficulties with reading scripture. Theologian and bishop Augustine
himself, in his *Confessions*, depicted scripture as forests or dark
thickets, difficult to navigate. Reading scripture has enough
minefields to discourage the most intrepid seeker. The biggest
hindrance, though, is if we refuse to recognize the problems
inherent in sacred texts.

I once met a woman who criticized Unitarian Universalism
because of a position she heard we had taken on the Israeli-
Palestinian situation. She launched into an impassioned explanation of how God had given the Hebrew people the land of
Israel for eternity, citing biblical texts to shore up her argument.

"But," I said, "we Unitarian Universalists don't take the Bible literally."

Her intensity melted away as she froze. After a moment, she collected her thoughts and replied, "No wonder you think what you do."

She recognized that her position absolutely depended on the literal truth of scripture. Absent that, she had no argument. Such overvaluation of a particular text makes life a challenge in a diverse, culturally and religiously rich world. Even a single text produces multiple meanings, depending either on the part of the book or the particular tradition of interpretation. Since Unitarian Universalists do not assign ultimate religious authority to any text, it's particularly helpful for us to understand some of the complexities of interpretation as we approach ancient scriptures that are central to the beliefs and practices of their adherents.

Interpretation

As noted earlier, there are many challenges related to scriptural interpretation: the perception of the authority of the text, the history of the text, how and why it came to be, who its writers and readers have been, how it's been read through the years, the contradictions found within the texts—all these influence and complicate interpretation. What's more, in spiritual reading, the focus may be less on the text itself than on the connection with the sacred that comes from reading the text. It may point to something beyond either the reader or the text. In that case, a reader may learn things about the self or the world that have little to do with the text or the tradition from which it comes.

It is also true that different traditions within a religion may have different ways of reading the same text. Each sect's adherents come to the page with a unique set of understandings informing them. Even when two people agree on the underpinnings, the life experiences they bring to the text may create differences in interpretation. This is true for Catholics and Protestants, for Sunni and Shi'a Muslims, for Mahayana and Theravada Buddhists, for Reform and Orthodox Jews, and for multiple types of Hindus. In short, texts don't mean the same thing, even within a religion.

Comparing interpretations can be like observing artists painting the same still life from their own unique perspectives and in different styles. Sometimes you wonder whether they are even talking about the same book. That can be a joy too, though. And it gives permission to the reader—because if people who have studied and pondered a book don't agree on its meaning, then we as readers can also bring what we have to the text and see where it takes us. Interpretation includes both scholarship—understanding the known facts about the scripture, its context, and its background—as well as art—making real what can only be imagined, not to mention whatever the movement of the spirit might bring.

However, every scriptural text should come with a warning label: USE WITH CAUTION.

Proof Texting

The practice of using a scriptural quotation alone to make an argument is common enough to have its own name: proof texting. Scriptures from any tradition can be applied to a situation without regard for context, scholarship, or nuances. But every book is more than a collection of isolated words, and we need to remember that as we engage with it.

The Protestant foundation of *sola scriptura*, "scripture alone," articulated by Martin Luther, laid the groundwork for controversy about biblical meaning. If we attend only to scripture, then tradition or clerics do not have the authority to tell regular people what the Bible, or God, means. The early twentieth-century development of fundamentalism in Protestant Christianity built walls around the Good Book, insisting on a literal reading. Fundamentalist Protestants view the Bible as not just central and sacred, but as inerrant and literally true. While a literal approach to the Bible does not necessarily deny the allegories and metaphors that it includes, such a limited view can result in rhetorical gymnastics and denials of science.

This particular approach to the Bible has made proof texting a special problem in conservative Protestantism. Often, the proof texters are already convinced of their particular point of view. When they stumble across an authority, a scripture, that seems to agree with them, they embrace that passage and spout it as evidence. One result can be a sermon filled with scriptural allusions that have no relation to one another but, strung together, create a web of an argument for the preacher's position. It could look a bit like Jewish *midrash*, which strings together verses from various places to develop an argument. *Midrash*, though, rarely insists on a single point of view, instead spreading out the various arguments and allowing readers some space to make up their own minds. The proof-texted argument, though, denies truth outside of the argument from scripture.

Another effect of the practice can be the dueling proof text:

One person says, "You shall not lie with a male as with a woman; it is an abomination" (Leviticus 18:22). Then they are countered by another person, who says, "But if you are led by the Spirit, you are not subject to the law" (Galatians 5:18).

The first arguer fires back from Romans 1:26–27: "Their women exchanged natural intercourse for unnatural, and in the same way also the men, giving up natural intercourse with women, were consumed with passion for one another. Men committed shameless acts with men and received in their own persons the due penalty for their error."

To which the reply comes: "Do not judge, so that you may not be judged" (Matthew 7:1).

Such arguments cannot be won. If one takes scripture as authority, the only way to delve into the muck is to look more closely at the context of each of the verses.

As evangelical professor Donald Carson quotes his minister father, "a text without a context is a pretext for a proof text."[35] In other words, removing phrases, sentences, and even paragraphs from their original context can obscure, distort, or disguise their true meaning. Context includes the written words around the piece and the historical development and traditional use of the text. Quoting a bit of scripture doesn't prove anything at all, especially an argument. That is why so much of the argument around scriptural interpretation ends up being about the context—when the book was written and the circumstances the author faced. If interpreters disagree on such basics, they will read the passage differently.

Though Protestant fundamentalists' view of scripture may encourage proof texting, they're not the only ones who do it. Anyone who pulls out a quotation to make a point, while diminishing or dismissing the context of the excerpt, is proof texting. This is particularly easy to do when one has only a passing familiarity with a text—or is relying on Wikiquotes! In today's fast-paced culture, skimming the surface has become commonplace, and distorting a religious tradition can be easier than we realize. This also applies to the texts that Unitarian Universalist communities sometimes treat in a scriptural way, such as the words of a social justice hero. In fact, we may be even more prone to do so because we assume more readily that we understand the meanings of such texts. To properly respect the religious texts we value, we must avoid proof texting and instead study the text to fully understand context and the richness of what the author and the tradition are saying. Of course, being outside a text's original context, we may never fully understand or appreciate it. The goal is to come closer, not to arrive.

Plain Sense

Much has been said about the "plain sense" meaning of text, usually making the argument that a text means what it appears to mean. All that we have discussed so far shows the fallacy of that understanding. First, readers always bring with them their backgrounds, preconceptions, and personal histories. If those packs full of biases do not line up exactly with those of authors of the text, it can lead to a misreading of the text. We are apt to read into a text what we want to see, rather than what is there.

If we can miss colleagues' jokes in an email and misinterpret them, how much more can we miss the meaning from an author we don't know, whose culture is distant in time and space? Though a text may seem to have a clear meaning, closer examination may turn it on its ear.

Culture Clashes

The form of family and the social order is reflected in the texts that come from a society. Often religious texts assume or even justify relationships that we might find unjust—slavery, seeing women and children as property, castes. Through time, people within religious traditions have questioned and resisted many of these justifications, leading to change. Of course, all traditions include people who resist change as well, clinging to old ways of being.

As we study texts, keep in mind the complexity within the tradition in its view of social problems. I may wince at the expectations of Confucius regarding filial piety, but when I study the chaotic times in which he lived, I understand the drive to assert order. I also gain insight into the Taoist responses and rejections of some Confucian admonitions. I strive to resist the temptation to oversimplify and condemn a text for the shortcomings and disappointments that come from the preconceptions I carry.

The Problem of Violence

Because scriptures address and include the people involved in the religious traditions, the problems of human experience sneak in. Sometimes, texts disappoint us because their own words seem to break from what we might expect. When we see violence in scripture that generally is considered to be sacred and having high moral standards, it takes us aback. Yet, many stories and sagas drip with blood and have inspired warfare through the centuries. I remember the incredulity of some students at Harvard Divinity School when they discovered the bloody warfare of the biblical books of Joshua and Judges. It countered their ideas of what their religion was. What are we to make of violence in scripture?

In the Bhagavad-Gita, a small section of the epic Mahabharata, the events take place as men prepare for battle. Though the fight can be explained as spiritual warfare, the text depicts a literal battlefield where Arjuna confronts his own relatives whom he does not wish to kill. The God Krishna, appearing as Arjuna's charioteer, persuades Arjuna that he must do his duty and engage in the battle. How can we overlook the violence of the setting and, indeed, of Krishna's insistence that Arjuna fight? Doesn't engaging in warfare contradict the religious impulse, especially when faced by an army of one's own family? Mahatma Gandhi himself struggled with this question:

Let it be granted that, according to the letter of the *Gita*, it is possible to say that warfare is consistent with renunciation of fruit. But after forty years' unremitting endeavor fully to enforce the teaching of the *Gita* in my own life, I have, in all humility, felt that perfect renunciation is impossible without perfect observance of *ahimsa* [not harming; non-violence] in every shape and form.[36]

Summarizing Gandhi's thought on the subject, or that of anyone who has spent extensive time studying the text, presents only a hint of how to understand. What more profound situation could one find oneself in than the one Arjuna is in? Thus, it is the perfect opportunity to find what is most profound in life. The story includes inner spiritual turmoil depicted by the encounter of Krishna with Arjuna, the divinity within confronting the human being, exploring the *atman* and *Brahman* and their relation. The story raises the issue of duty, following expectations and laws without question. The symbolism sewn into the situation provides the opportunity to explore some of the deepest questions of human existence.

In fact, human life seems inevitably to include violence and war. No culture has escaped it entirely, either as victims or perpetrators. Violence and how to respond to it are firmly established aspects of life; people have always had to struggle with them and likely always will. What is our duty in war? How do we relate to perpetrators of crime? How do we deal with the urge to commit violence? These are religious and spiritual questions, so of course, scriptures throughout the ages have included perplexing passages about violence.

Similarly, violence rears its head in the Qur'an, in the Hebrew Scriptures, and in the writings of the Tenth Nanak of Sikhism, to name a few. Scripture includes violence and war because they are human problems that people must struggle to deal with through their religious traditions. Scriptures that ignore human problems such as slavery, political oppression, crime, and punishment would be superficial because they fail to address the real social challenges of religious adherents. Do the scriptures sometimes get it wrong? As Unitarian Universalists we have the freedom to say, yes, sometimes, they do. After all, they were written by human beings. But including the hard parts of human life is no error—and sometimes, they offer us ways to encounter the tough realities of human living.

Cultural Misappropriation

Religious borrowing has a long and complex history. Jews adapted texts from the Babylonians and Egyptians. The Romans imported stories from the Greeks. The Qur'an draws on Jewish and Christian stories. Buddhism learned from the Vedas, though they ended up setting them aside. In China, Confucianism, Taoism, and Buddhism simmered in a religious stew.

Unitarian Universalists, drawing as we do from a wide variety of sources, face a special challenge when it comes to cultural misappropriation—the practice of inappropriately using materials or practices from another culture for our own purposes. Because Unitarian Universalists do not have a canon of our own, and our tradition has moved away from the use of the books that our founders saw as holy, we have often crossed cultural barriers; we will continue to do so. The question is, how do we cross those barriers while adhering to our values, being respectful, seeking truth, and not taking what does not belong to us?

Our dilemma is further complicated by the complexity of backgrounds from which Unitarian Universalists come. Unitarian Universalist Jews, Buddhists, or Native Americans may carry with them rituals, music, or texts from their upbringing that they would like to incorporate in their UU context. However, they are surrounded by people for whom these practices are unfamiliar.

There are Unitarian Universalist Buddhists, for example, for whom the Lotus Sutra has deep and special meaning. They will have a different approach to studying that sutra than Unitarian Universalists who have no Buddhist connection. They may chant the sutra in a phonetic approximation of Sanskrit, which could be a practice that would be foreign, and perhaps inappropriate, for a Unitarian Universalist who didn't find meaning and personal connection in the sutra.

Over the last thirty years, Unitarian Universalists have begun to think more carefully about the dilemma. The late Marjorie Bowens-Wheatley, an African-American Unitarian Universalist minister, writes about it this way:

> We intentionally seek to learn about world religions and to share other cultural rituals and traditions. We lack depth, however, in our understanding of the historical, racial, cultural and religious context, as well as sensitivity to these

contexts. At worst, our approach is assimilation, a combination of voyeurism and thievery, which in effect seems to say: from the distance of time and space, we have permission to take a myopic look at whatever culture we choose, and to beg, borrow or steal whatever we like, and make it our own.[37]

Power dynamics are key to the issue. If we, as a largely white, privileged group, use our privilege to take others' traditions and skew them to our own usage, removing them from their context, we are being insensitive and exploitative. If we approach sacred books from other traditions while continuing to believe that our own culture is superior—or is "normal," as opposed to a deviant culture of others—we do more than distort any truths that might be learned from what we read. Indeed, we disrespect a group of people.

While these challenges apply to all religious traditions, they may be most pronounced with indigenous forms of religious practice. While many of these may have no written scripture, they usually have oral texts—stories and rituals that have been handed down as sacred teaching that can be thought of as scripture because of their sacredness. Some people from these traditions are very protective of their stories, avoiding sharing them with people outside their ethnic group. Particular care should be taken to engage with people who practice the traditions from which you want to borrow rather than trying to study the sacred stories and rituals—or adopt them—isolated from their lived context. If we understand by engaging with people, we learn their rules and expectations of how their practices ought to be treated.

How, then, can we interact with texts and traditions in which we are not personally rooted? Invitation is a first step. If someone steeped in a cultural or religious tradition invites me to a ritual or celebration, my participation has been sanctioned. Of course, that doesn't mean I then make suggestions on how to carry it out or criticize the way it is done. Instead, I attend the event with as open a mind as possible, striving to learn from the culture into which I have been invited. As the event or ritual unfolds, I make sure at each step of the proceedings that my participation continues to be welcomed.

Books are a bit different. If a sacred text has been published, it is available to all who open it. Still, we can enter that text either with an attitude that we can do whatever we want with it, or we can read and study with our judgment suspended, with curiosity, and with a desire to learn. What's more, we can strive to understand the context fully, so that we can engage in a deep way.

Ideally, we can stay in relationship with the people who call these books sacred. Just as people working with contextual theologies need a covenantal relationship with a group to whom they are accountable, we need to be in relationship with people who call a book sacred if we are to really understand what it is about. This is particularly true regarding traditions that have been oppressed by groups who hold the same identities that we do. Rather than perpetuate the structures of oppression, we work toward solidarity with those who have been oppressed.

This standard makes sense for the way we should engage with the scriptures of all other religions as well. We need to work to connect with practitioners of the religion, to understand their use of texts and what they consider appropriate to share. When something develops meaning for us and we learn about it in depth, we may be able to engage with it in a new way.

As we engage with a text—whether it is considered sacred or not in the eyes of the people who created it—we may find it taking on richer meaning. Our study and use of it in worship may lead us to view it as sacred.

Healthy doses of humility, curiosity, and respect go a long way. The key may be to always know who we are, and always respect who others are, treasuring both what we share and the ways in which we are different and can learn from one another.

Nowhere is the problem of misappropriation more prevalent than it is regarding Native American traditions. The people who lived on this continent prior to European conquest had complex theological understandings based in story and ritual, which they did not label separately as "religious," but which they lived. Those cultural backgrounds, including language, came under siege through overt and covert forms of violence. From Indian wars to Indian schools, whites worked to subvert, erase, and eliminate native people and their ways of understanding the world. Yet, some of those cultures survived. Native people today are reclaiming them. The oppression and extermination experienced by native people makes claims on Native American spirituality and stories by whites particularly egregious. Care must be exercised. The passage at the end of this chapter examines a text that has elicited mixed reactions from both white and native readers.

The Challenge of Comprehension

Contemporary Western Buddhist David Chapman blogged:

> I've forced myself to read some [Buddhist scripture]. Almost all of it is exceedingly boring. It's unbelievably repetitive, it takes a full page to make a simple point that could be said in a sentence, and most of it is just silly, one way or another.
>
> And then, there's large chunks that are hopelessly obscure. Often, oral tradition agrees that they are incomprehensible; no one claims to be sure what they mean.
>
> Occasionally you learn something—but you have to be a masochist.[38]

The idea that scripture is repetitive, silly, obscure, and even incomprehensible can certainly be found among Unitarian Universalists. But we must consider what those scriptures mean for the adherents of the traditions they represent. Much of scripture, especially if it was originally oral, is boring and repetitive to modern ears. Oral works developed repetition to help make memorization easier. Scripture can be very difficult to understand. Words, grammar, and structure have evolved even since the nineteenth century; how can we hope to relate to vocabulary and grammatical constructions that come from a couple thousand years ago, from cultures different than our own? How can we relate to scriptures so complex that various sects or schools argue shades of meanings of words, or sometimes even letters, or the curlicues attached to the letters? Why would any sane person even engage in such a practice? Masochism sounds like a reasonable explanation.

Yet, these texts have survived the centuries. Millions of people have found something in them: inspiration, challenge, motivation, encouragement, meaning, maybe even something ultimate, perhaps a road to God. They have met the test of time. They have crossed cultural barriers. They have survived.

Understanding isn't easy. We have to overcome multiple barriers and resist the temptation to think we understand more than we do. Scripture reading should not be done glibly or taken lightly.

To really begin to understand scripture requires disciplined study, an attitude of humility, and a willingness to ask people who know more than you do—you don't have to accept their interpretation, but their input can provide valuable guidance.

Perspective and Place

Reading scriptures may be rewarding and educational, and even bring us closer to the divine. However, we must keep them in perspective. Addison Hodges Hart, college chaplain and writer, in discussing the Ox Herder drawings from Chinese Zen Buddhism, remarks,

> Scriptures and teachings are very important for finding enlightenment or God. But the tracks are not the Ox, and the scriptures are not substitutes for enlightenment or God. They are not ends in themselves. They won't last forever. Tracks can be washed away by a rainstorm. Tracks can even mislead us if we're not wise in the ways of how to read them

with accuracy. Similarly, scriptures are signs; but what we search for is reality, the goal.[39]

Hart suggests that scripture reading, then, is not an end in itself. Certainly, we have seen how the question of accuracy is not as easy as it might appear, given the diversity of interpretations with which it is read. As for reality, it may be a goal, but it is ever an elusive one. Scripture may offer us knowledge about our neighbors or point us toward God or lead us to enlightenment. Readers need to stay aware of their own particular goals, while being open to something completely unexpected. Scriptures are nothing but a tool—a valuable tool, but never an end in themselves.

A Reading from Black Elk Speaks, Being the Life Story of a Holy Man of the Oglala Sioux

And as I looked and wept, I saw that there stood on the north side of the starving camp a sacred man who was painted red all over his body, and he held a spear as he walked into the center of the people, and there he lay down and rolled. And when he got up, it was a fat bison standing there, and where the bison stood a sacred herb sprang up right where the tree had been in the center of the nation's hoop. The herb grew and bore four blossoms on a single stem while I was looking— a blue, a white, a scarlet, and a yellow—and the bright rays of these flashed to the heavens.

I know now what this meant, that the bison were the gift of a good spirit and were our strength, but we should lose them, and from the same good spirit we must find another strength. For the people all seemed better when the herb had grown and bloomed, and the horses raised their tails and neighed and pranced around, and I could see a light breeze going from the north among the people like a ghost; and suddenly the flowering tree was

there again at the center of the nation's hoop
where the four-rayed herb had blossomed.[40]

> As told through John G. Neihardt
> (Flaming Rainbow)

THIS IS AN UNCONVENTIONAL TEXT. Rather than dating back
to the dawn of time, it was first published in 1932. However,
the symbols and stories referenced in the work date to an
unknown time, transmitted orally through the Lakota nation.
The scholar and activist Vine Deloria Jr. (Lakota), called
it "perhaps the only religious classic of this [the twentieth]
century."[41] Yet, other Native Americans have scoffed at the
idea that it is truly native, given that the published book was
a white man's interpretation of Black Elk's words. Of course,
Native Americans belong to a variety of nations or tribes and
thus have no universal canon. Though united in recognizing
the connectedness of all creation and understanding a unity in
spirit, mind, emotion, and body, each particular nation draws
on its own, primarily oral tradition as authoritative in ethical and liturgical matters. Many would argue against the term
"scripture" at all in these traditions. For that matter, Native
Americans might not separate these ideas out as religious or
secular, seeing no such separation of spheres of life. However,
a Unitarian Universalist community might find such deep wisdom in this passage that they engage with it in a scriptural
way. In such a case, out of respect they would be obliged to try
to understand the origins of the passage, how it is received in
the community it purports to represent, and the cultural context that underlies it.

Black Elk Speaks conveys something of the Lakota tradition. Lakota symbols and stories permeate Black Elk's mystical
experience. Much of traditional knowledge is carefully guarded
and less accessible than this recounting. This particular book,
though, came when traditional knowledge had been severely
disrupted by conquest and oppression. *Black Elk Speaks* originates in a specific culture, from a defined group of people, with
a particular human dilemma, that of losing substantial parts
of Native American culture and life to invasion first by Europeans and then by white Americans. The pain, dislocation,
and historical trauma communicated in the passage demand
acknowledgment.

Controversy has swirled around the figures of Nicholas
Black Elk (Oglala Lakota) and John G. Neihardt in the
decades since the book's appearance. Black Elk himself was a
complicated figure. He served as a Catholic catechist, teaching
Catholicism, but always retained his Lakota spiritual identity.
His alliance with and agreement to work with Niehardt precipitated a range of responses from native people. At the same
time, Black Elk has been recognized as a prophet and religious
leader by other Native Americans.

In a sense, the two collaborated to produce the book, with
the assistance of Black Elk's son, Ben, who served as translator, and Neihardt's daughter, Enid, who wrote the English
translations in shorthand and later transcribed them. Scholars
who have compared the published book to the recorded tran-
scriptions find that Neihardt took liberties with Black Elk's
words, elaborating some of the historical and cultural context,
omitting some of the war imagery, and making the text more

universalistic. However, even some of the most rigorous critics continue to find the book inspiring as it was written.

Who were these two men? Nicholas Black Elk was an Oglala Lakota Wicasa Wakan (holy man). Though he had converted to Catholicism, perhaps as a survival strategy, he remained inspired by visions that came to him beginning in his childhood, and he believed the traditional ways needed to be preserved and recorded for the world. Second cousin and friend to Crazy Horse, Black Elk was recognized as a medicine man by the age of 19. He lived through the Battle of Little Bighorn and the Wounded Knee Massacre and traveled with Buffalo Bill's Wild West Show. John G. Neihardt, a white man, was poet laureate of Nebraska and a student of Native American culture and history. He met Black Elk as he was researching the Ghost Dance, a widespread spiritual movement among various Indian nations, including the Lakota, throughout the West during the late nineteenth century. Adopted as son by Black Elk and given the name Flaming Rainbow after an image in Black Elk's Great Vision, Neihardt became the one to record the spiritual content Black Elk felt compelled to disclose. According to contemporaries, the men seemed to share a mystical union in which they understood more than they spoke aloud.

Black Elk Speaks comes from a series of meetings between the two men from August 1930 through May 1931. With the translator and transcriber, this might seem an unlikely way to create scripture, yet it's not the first time that someone transcribed visions and teachings from another person. The greatest challenge is that, in this case, the transcriber and the prophet came from different cultures, but together crafted a text that many consider sacred and that gives insight into Lakota life-ways and the lived experience of Black Elk.

Black Elk introduces Neihardt—and through him, the world—to an Other World outside the concrete visible sphere, a world of spirit. The selection that may be most widely recognized from *Black Elk Speaks* appears in *Singing the Living Tradition* as "The Sacred Hoop," Number 614. However, that text has been criticized as having universalistic interpretations added by Neihardt. Instead, I have selected another piece of Black Elk's Great Vision to consider. This passage reports both a slice of the vision and Black Elk's interpretation of that vision.

When the passage begins, Black Elk has just witnessed his people of all ages making a difficult journey upward through four levels. They had turned into animals at one point, but now had shifted back into people, who were starving, as were their horses. And their sacred flowering tree had disappeared. Even the narrator in his vision sobs. No wonder Black Elk finds himself crying (". . . as I looked and wept"). The vision reflects the real trauma Black Elk's people were in the midst of, losing their cultural connections and their livelihood.

Yet this part of the vision ultimately presents us with an image of the resilience and adaptability of the Lakota, and the persistent presence for them of the sacredness of the natural world. The context of the Lakota grounds the symbolic under-standings of Black Elk's experience. Several images stand out in this passage and connect with Lakota tradition. Black Elk deciphers some of the images right in the passage, while others carry traditional symbolism that is not shared here. The man who appears at the beginning is red, the color of first light, placing him in the creation story. His transformation to a bison also echoes the creation story. As Black Elk implies in the interpretation, bison were essential to the people, and their loss was devastating. The bison, Black Elk tells us, are disappearing, yet the herb that grows represents something new given to the people.

Significantly, the sacred herb, and later, the flowering tree, spring from the center of the hoop, representing holistic balance. The herb is four-rayed, consistent with the four directions, with blue representing the West, white the North, red the East, and yellow the South,[42] and they are joined together on a single stem, showing their unity. The ghost-like breeze from the north echoes the Ghost Dance. While the Ghost Dance was not a traditional aspect of the vision, the hint of its presence reflects Black Elk's own ambivalent relationship to this innovation by the Paiute Wovoka in the late nineteenth century. The breeze comes from the North, the place of spiritual guidance or the wisdom of the ancestors, so the flowering tree is their gift to the people, as the Ghost Dance was, despite its apparent failure as a movement.

The wholeness represented in the different directions may be part of what allows the flowering tree to reappear. The flowering tree symbolizes hope despite all the trials and difficulties that the people have endured. Black Elk's vision recognizes the challenges the people have faced, but insists that they will triumph and the hoop of the world will be restored. Even the horses will be happy when it comes.

That a man who had been physically present at the Wounded Knee massacre still found hope decades later, not so much for himself as for his people, speaks volumes about the resilience provided by spiritual centeredness. If we read this text carefully we can avoid romanticizing it or glibly universalizing it. We are reminded of the particularity of the context and are confronted by the results of oppression, even as the resilience of a culture shines through. Understanding how it was created prevents us from assigning it too much authority as a representation of a people and a culture. *Black Elk Speaks* is a complex, very useful example of a text often regarded as sacred, but that can be misread or oversimplified out of context, and how learning more about the text enriches understanding.

PART III

Using Scripture

CHAPTER NINE

Study

> ... The sacrifice to the Brahman is one's own
> study ...
>
> Satapatha Brahmana 11.5.6.3,
> translated by Julius Eggeling

THE EIGHTEENTH-CENTURY German playwright and philosopher Gotthold Lessing wrote words I have taken as guidance through much of my life: "I am not a scholar, I have never intended to be a scholar; I could not be a scholar, even if it were possible in a dream. All that I have made some small attempt to achieve is the ability to use a learned book in case of necessity." We should all be able to use a learned book—or tackle a scriptural text—if we need to. The word *study* means a variety of things when it comes to looking at books, including scripture. For some, scripture study means finding the divine guidance for our lives hidden—or laid out clearly—in a text. For others, study involves an academic pursuit: When and where was this written, and what did it mean for the people who were its initial audience? What has it meant through the ages?

Other parts of this book explore approaches to scripture study that come from sources outside Unitarian Universalism, such as the use of historical-critical study and *lectio divina*. Here, the focus is on study in Unitarian Universalist congregations.

Adult Religious Education

Adult learners seek engagement as much as they do information. If they want to learn about a text, there are plenty of ways to dig in, whether through books, university classes, or the Internet. When they come to congregationally based adult religious education classes, they are often looking for engagement with that text.

Scripture study can be offered for an hour on Sunday mornings, as often happens in the southern United States; in a weeknight series; or through a long-term, small-group format. A variety of teaching methods may be used. The method depends on what we are trying to understand: the origins of the text, what it means to current practitioners of a particular faith, or what it might mean to us as religious seekers. Engagement can be part of all those practices, both with the text itself, and with others who are also engaging with the text.

A frequent goal for a class is to acquaint participants with a diversity of religious perspectives in an effort to better understand the complexity of our world. The challenge is to communicate the breadth and depth of a tradition in a relatively short time. Whenever we summarize and generalize about a religious text, we have to keep in mind that many have spent their entire lives wrestling with a text that we are only touch-

ing on in an hour or two. We are barely glimpsing the wholeness of a scripture's truth, grappling with only a tiny piece of
a tradition—which is not to recommend against it! We will
know even less without making the attempt, but we have to
maintain perspective and humility.

How, then, do we introduce Unitarian Universalists to a
rainbow of different religious texts? A survey course, such as
Eternally Compelling (eternallycompelling.org), may be the eas-
iest approach. Developed by Unitarian Universalist scholars
at the First Unitarian Universalist Church of Nashville, the
curriculum provides a structure for exploring texts from Buddhism, Hinduism, Taoism, and Confucianism, as well as the
Abrahamic faiths.

Many UU churches have also studied Huston Smith's
works, especially *The World's Religions*, originally titled *The
Religions of Man*. While Smith doesn't engage primarily with
scriptures, a class could read together some piece of each religion's written texts as they study that tradition.

Sometimes, the focus may be on a particular text, in order
to better understand one specific religion. For example, some
non-Muslims have committed to reading the Qur'an during
Ramadan. Such study should always include background information on the religion, and interaction with one or more adherents of the faith. Scripture only makes sense within a context.
The reading at the end of this chapter will look at how a passage from the Dhammapada helps give insights into the Buddhist tradition.

To fully tap the wisdom of different traditions, we need to
go beyond academic study. Such exploration requires more
than a simple translation. Engagement with people steeped in

the tradition may help. If one of the goals is to find truths that speak to *us* from different religions, we'll want to sit with the text spiritually. That might involve experiencing the text as it is practiced by that religious tradition, listening to it being chanted, for example, in a temple or *sangha*. It might demand a close reading, and exploration of terms or words that stand out—*hesed* in the Hebrew Scriptures, or *dukkha* in a Buddhist text. How might these terms, foreign to us, live in our own lives and experiences?

How might we approach that in a class? Consider the word *hesed*. Rendered by interpreters as "compassion," "lovingkindness," "mercy," "steadfast love," and even as "loyalty," *hesed* doesn't translate easily into English. It implies not a one-way relationship, as in "I love you," but a secure mutuality in which parties do for one another freely and out of love. More than an emotion, *hesed* describes a commitment. To explore the meaning of *hesed*, the class could read a story together in which *hesed* is central, such as the story of Ruth's refusal to leave her mother-in-law Naomi. The class could consider the various translations of the word, then discuss in groups of two or three when they have experienced *hesed* in their own lives. Finally, the group might discuss how they would translate the word. What English word or phrase best captures the sentiment expressed in the Hebrew *hesed*?

When we combine the use of a text, foreign or familiar, with our own experience, we begin to grasp how reading scripture can influence our lives. On the other hand, if we are seeking to understand how scripture affects other people, the adherents of a particular faith, our time is better spent interacting with those people about the application of scripture to their lives. So, if the goal is to learn more about what the text means to people from a particular tradition, we need to invite those people to speak, or go to their communities in an effort to learn from them.

Small Group Study

A few individuals might want to devote themselves to a particular text for an extended period of time. In one church I served, a covenant group studied the Upanishads over the course of several months. Other groups might want to read the lectionary together. Though several versions exist, the Revised Common Lectionary selects texts from both the Hebrew Bible and New Testament that are often read in the worship context by several different Protestant denominations. A group might take an in-depth look at the selections, either with the aid of a curriculum like *The Bible Workbench* (educationalcenter.org/about/our-publications/subscribe-bibleworkbench), which many Unitarian Universalists have found useful, or through developing their own questions and discussion points.

A committed small group studying together gains more than insight into the text. By struggling together with the challenges of translations, interpretations, and experience, group members encounter themselves and one another in new ways. An expanded sense of connection invites more vulnerability and, potentially, greater transformation.

In recent years, Abrahamic faiths have done more to try to understand each other through small groups including a diversity of members. Curricula have been developed, such as

For One Great Peace: An Interfaith Study Guide, from the Abrahamic Faiths Peacemaking Initiative (abrahamicfaiths peacemaking.com/wp-content/uploads/2012/10/For-One-Great-Peace-Study-Guide.pdf). Similarly, the 2006 publication of *The Faith Club: A Muslim, a Christian, a Jew—Three Women Search for Understanding*, a book by three women of different faiths, encouraged formation of other small groups to explore across traditions, delving into the shared and unshared scriptures of three traditions.

Getting involved in interfaith efforts in the community may produce opportunities to do structured study together. The work is tender, as disagreements around scripture and its application have precipitated literal battles in the history of the world. Yet, if such differences are ever to be mended, individual relationships may provide the pathway.

Children and Youth

The renowned Unitarian religious educator Sophia Fahs argued that children shouldn't be exposed to Bible stories until well along in elementary school. Fahs had been raised by evangelical Christian missionaries and felt the immersion in the biblical story had harmed her own spiritual and religious development.

Yet, children thrive on stories and make sense of the world through them. Though adults may do to same, the stories introduced to children may provide the lenses they use throughout their lifetimes in making sense of the world. Children need to learn the "big stories" of our culture so that they feel connected and have a library of experience to draw on as they go through life. Exposure to religious scriptures should be primarily through story before and during elementary school. As abstract abilities begin to develop, other concepts from religious traditions can be introduced. Teenagers frequently enjoy exploration of unfamiliar faiths. Relating them to our Unitarian Universalist history and tradition enlivens both. Youth classes could compare Emerson's Over-soul to the Hindu view of Brahman, for example.

Many traditional religious stories include topics that may not be developmentally appropriate for younger children. Yet, the need to begin to figure out how they relate to family and peers, to hurting and helping, to emotions and thought, even to disease and death, starts even before school does.

We cannot guess how a young child will hear and understand a story. Once in a worship service, I told a story about a spider that laid its eggs, then died. A four-year-old whose mother was pregnant then feared that her mother would die after having the baby. Another time, a father came to me, concerned about his asthmatic seven-year-old. The boy, a firstborn child, had been hospitalized and close to death. When he heard the Passover story, where the Hebrews had marked their lintels with blood so the angel of death would avoid taking their firstborn, he became convinced that his parents needed to put blood over their door to keep him from dying.

These are cautionary anecdotes, not arguments against telling children stories. Children may come up with their own interpretations of stories, interpretations that seem silly or farfetched to grown-ups. Adults need to supplement the storytelling, guiding children to discern helpful, realistic interpretations and away from scary or overly imaginative ones. Listening to young people's questions and taking seriously their concerns help our children develop the skills to make meaning in their lives, including making meaning out of scripture.

Unitarian Universalist churches always have a cohort of children whose first question is, "Is that real?" At different ages, though, different views of "truth" emerge. Developmentally, young elementary students are sorting out truth from fiction and have trouble understanding that a truth can be metaphorical. Preschool children, on the other hand, may not grasp that there is any difference between reality and a good story. They are immersed in a magical world. And why not? If you don't understand the science and technology behind them, electricity and indoor plumbing look like magic, not to mention computer tablets.

Stories, whether coming from scripture or other sources, need context. With children, a storyteller may want to declare whether the story could really happen, or tell about the people who believe the story is true. Rather than associating it with a particular religion, children might want to hear where the story comes from in the world or how old it is. Older stories have a patina of enchantment, like a dream. Hearing stories from a variety of perspectives helps children know that different cultures and ways of thinking exist.

Youth have developed abstract thought and learned that people differ in their cultural backgrounds and approaches. They will be particularly interested in different ways of doing religion. Unitarian Universalists have long introduced young teens to different faiths, using curricula such as *The Church Across the Street* and *Neighboring Faiths*, as well as the current *Building Bridges* curriculum, which is part of *Tapestry of Faith*, available online at uua.org. *Building Bridges* looks at a variety of scriptures, including Hebrew and Christian scriptures, the Qur'an, the Bhagavad-Gita, the Tao Te Ching, and the Dhammapada.

Whatever the age, reading scripture together, voicing our thoughts and ideas about it, and finding out how others have interpreted it through the ages can enrich our lives. Many texts, such as the Dhammapada, tell us something about what study can mean.

A Reading from Dhammapada

We are what we think.
All that we are arises with our thoughts.
With our thoughts we make the world. Speak or
　act with an impure mind
And trouble will follow you
As the wheel follows the ox that draws the cart.

We are what we think.
All that we are arises with our thoughts.
With our thoughts we make the world. Speak or
　act with a pure mind
And happiness will follow you
As your shadow, unshakable.

　　　　　Dhammapada 1:1–2, translated by Thomas Byrom

AMONG THE MOST esteemed texts in Buddhism, the Dhammapada includes teachings originally given by the Buddha, reportedly on three hundred or more different occasions. *Dhamma* is Pali for *dharma*, or "teachings," and *pada* implies "path" or "way."

Soon after Buddha's death in the fifth century BCE, hundreds of his disciples gathered at the First Council at Rajagaha and put together his sayings and sermons in an oral collection that they memorized. The resulting canon, called the Tipitaka in the Pali language, includes the Dhammapada, which is considered one of the "little texts." We don't know how long the oral dharma circulated and how it evolved, but tradition tells us the scriptures were written on palm leaves following another Buddhist council around the first century BCE. The text appears in various languages and versions, though the Pali version is most often referenced.

The book may be the most concise and accessible summary of Buddhist teachings, and most Buddhist groups revere it. Buddhist teacher and translator Acharya Buddharaskkhita calls it the "best known and most widely esteemed text in the Pali Tipitaka."[43] With numerous English translations from as early as the nineteenth century, Westerners—Buddhist and non-Buddhist—have long studied it.

The Text

The excerpt above comprises the first two verses of the Dhammapada. The line "All that we are arises with our thoughts" offers a radically non-materialistic view of the world. The world, according to this passage, depends not on some objective standard of reality, but on what goes on in each person's mind. We become responsible for what Buddhists call "right thought." Suffering occurs not because of what we endure, but because of how we think about what we endure.

The repetition in the passage reminds us of its origin as oral text, but also reinforces and strengthens the force of the meaning. Different translators render the words in different points of view. This particular translation uses first person plural, but other translations use second person, third person, or no personal pronouns at all! The perspective may influence how the reader relates to the passage, or fails to, but the meaning is the same.

The upshot is that when a person's mind is set on a particular object or belief, it becomes a stronger reality for that person. Much of Buddhism concerns the training of the mind.

The metaphors in the passage bring the meaning to life. The ox drags the cart, and the wheel of the cart follows the foot of the ox. In the same way, trouble and suffering follow an impure mind. One's shadow sticks as closely to the body as happiness does to a pure mind. The pictures provide additional clarity. But what do the concepts mean? What is an impure mind? What is happiness? What is a clear mind? More study is required. Again, different translators give us different ideas. For example, "impure mind" is also called "evil thought" (as translated by Ekneth Easwaren and Max Müller) or "corrupted heart" (as translated by Thanissaro Bhikkhu). To understand, we have to consider the larger world of dharma.

Buddhist Teachings

Buddhism teaches four noble truths:

1. Suffering (*dukkha*) exists.
2. The source of suffering is craving, or desire.
3. Suffering can be ended by letting go of craving.

4. The way to stop craving and suffering is through the Eightfold Path.

The Eightfold Path consists of right view, right intention,
right speech, right action, right livelihood, right effort, right
mindfulness, and right concentration. Right speech and right
action are connected to the words of the text: "When I speak
or act with a clear awareness." Of course, the various compo-
nents of the Eightfold Path strengthen and interrelate with
one another. How can I speak or act rightly without setting my
mind to do so through mindfulness and concentration? We see
here the Buddhist focus on training the mind.

   Buddhism has always been a practical religion. The Buddha
himself told potential practitioners to try his approach and see
if it worked and only stick with it if it did. Today, research con-
firms at least some of what Buddha taught (see Rick Hanson's
and Richard Mendius' book, *Buddha's Brain: The Practical Neuroscience of Happiness, Love and Wisdom*). These first two verses
of the Dhammapada tell us the basis of the teaching: Begin
with the mind. Focus the mind and happiness will eventually
follow.

The Dhammapada and Unitarian Universalism

The previous chapter explored the search for intersections
between our own experiences as Unitarian Universalists and
those of other religious traditions. We can consider the Dhammapada with this in mind. Like Buddhism, Unitarian Universalism has always been practical, focusing on this world rather

than the next and applying tests of experience and reason to its practices and teachings. Since the time of the Transcendentalists, Buddhism has resonated for Unitarians and Unitarian Universalists.

This particular teaching about the power of the mind to control and create our reality, or at least our interpretation of reality, helps in our understanding of our experiences. I can imagine a Unitarian Universalist class exploring the passage with questions like these:

- Do you agree or disagree with the Dhammapada about the power of thought?
- How do suffering and happiness relate to your state of mind?
- Have you ever changed your mind about the interpretation of an event and found yourself more content as a result?

CHAPTER TEN

Scripture in Worship

> This house is for the ingathering of nature and
> human nature. . . . It is a house of truth-seeking,
> where scientists can encourage devotion to their
> quest, where mystics can abide in a community
> of searchers. It is a house of art, adorning its
> celebrations with melodies and handiworks. It is
> a house of prophecy, outrunning times past and
> times present in visions of growth and progress.
> This house is a cradle for our dreams, the workshop
> of our common endeavor.
>
> Kenneth L. Patton, Unitarian Universalist

WORSHIP OFFERS the central communal experience in our congregations. The UUA bylaws even dictate that a Unitarian Universalist congregation must have regular religious services in order to maintain its connection with the UUA. Though we might not always agree on the purpose of worship, on what we are worshipping—or even that we *are* worshipping!—we all recognize the centrality of the gathering called worship, or service, or by some other name.

Most Unitarian Universalist services follow the practice of including readings as an aspect of worship, as is common in many religious traditions. Christians, Jews, and most Buddhists do the same. In contrast to non-UU services, though, the readings are not from a single source such as the Bible, but range across religious traditions, cultures, and eras. Often, we tend toward contemporary readings, eschewing older, more traditional sources. Readings may be song lyrics or newspaper articles, dictionary definitions, essays, poetry, or practically anything that has been written. Sometimes, they are scripture.

Thinking of scripture only as potential readings, though, limits its influence in creating the transformational experience that we hope worship can be. Scripture can show up in places other than the "readings" slot of the order of the service and can guide us into deeper understanding and connection. Whatever its place in the liturgy, scripture can be a vital part of our religious services.

Readings Versus Scripture

Authority, as acknowledged early in this book, is a tricky matter for Unitarian Universalists, and nowhere more complicated than in worship. With freedom of the pulpit, no one restricts a minister's right to determine themes or topics for preaching. The task of selecting readings for worship is beyond the scope of this book, but a limited look at scripture and its interaction with the service is in order.

Unitarian Universalists reject the notion that any particular text is infallible or essential to our spiritual development. Though we are not alone among religious adherents in that notion, we may be the most adamant about it. We believe that we can encounter the sacred in the secular world. When we select a reading for worship from *The Huffington Post*, we are demonstrating that. However, we are not necessarily elevating *The Huffington Post* to sacred text status. Not everything we read in worship is scripture.

Sometimes, though, we do read scripture in worship. How and why are significant questions. In *Worship That Works: Theory and Practice for Unitarian Universalists*, Wayne Arnason and Kathleen Rolenz describe three different ways of using readings in worship: adornment, companion, or spiritual guide. Scripture could make sense in any of those three usages.

A reading is an adornment when it hits the same theme or topic of the sermon but is not essential to the message of the sermon. Companion readings are more directly related; the sermon may quote the reading and the two dwell together, echoing ideas and reinforcing one another, stronger together than apart. Finally, the spiritual guide is integral to the sermon, as in lectionary preaching, which we will consider in the next section.

Drawing a reading from scripture—whether the Hebrew Scriptures, New Testament, or the Tao Te Ching—invites consideration of a truth that has endured through the ages. While scripture is not infallible, its staying power suggests usefulness. To use scripture thoughtfully, preacher and congregant alike allow it to soak into us and change our own ideas about the theme or topic. We wrestle with the scripture's meaning in our particular context.

Scripture in worship can hold a deeper resonance than a reading that may be heard only once. This only happens, though, if we are willing to repeat a particular reading regularly. Some of scripture's authority comes when familiarity and repetition transport us beyond the logical part of the brain and summon past associations with the text, whether or not we are aware of that mental process.

Unitarian Universalist worship planners draw from a huge variety of sources for readings. Christian-leaning congregations use the Bible regularly. Many of us, though, become enamored with what is new, neglecting the classics. Yet, these texts have formed societies and cultures and often provide more profound, if more difficult, truths. Some ministers even strive to read one ancient and one modern text each week, with ancient ones more likely to be scriptural.

How, then, do we use scripture as communal ritual in Unitarian Universalism? Well into the twentieth century, many of our churches included recitation of the Lord's Prayer in worship. Today, that is far less common. However, our use of responsive readings also brings in ritual. Even more, chalice lightings—even outside of worship—help define sacred space for religious education and meetings, and can use scriptural readings. We may want to consider how much we vary the words or keep the standard versions to have the meaning seep into participants. Using a single chalice lighting in various settings may be helpful in bringing sacred space from the sanctuary to meeting rooms and people's homes.

We also might want to try chant or communal prayer as meditative techniques in spiritual practice groups. Basing these in scripture could add a dimension to our experience, both of the technique and of the text. Of course, the cautions of respectful use apply here.

Scriptural Text as a Spiritual Guide

Most Unitarian Universalist preaching is not directly based on a scriptural text. That is, readings supplement or introduce the sermon, serving as adornment or companion rather than creating the context for the sermon. This practice contrasts with the traditional Christian congregation, where the sermon is expected to tie into and elaborate upon a biblical passage.

On the other hand, Mark Belletini, the minister emeritus of the First Unitarian Universalist Church of Columbus, said, "The way that I view the creation of worship as art form is to be an exegete of the readings—to weave the readings in and throughout the service and sermon. Sometimes, I'll take two readings and use one as the theme and the other reading as the motif, but they all must weave together as a whole."[44]

An exegete focuses attention on the passage, interpreting, developing, and applying it. That requires that the selection of the text comes before the sermon, or any other part of the service. Scripture may be the most appropriate kind of selection for such use, because the preacher in this case aims to develop something worthy of such intense attention, something that holds up to scrutiny and offers rewards for the work. Various methods may be applied to develop the meaning of the text or texts, including methods discussed earlier in this book. Helping the congregation understand the context of the reading, playing with its vocabulary or voice, calling on its use in spiritual practice, considering translations, looking for resonances, living its story—all this and more can be part of using a scriptural reading as a spiritual guide in preaching. The key is immersion in the text and seeing what comes out of it.

Repetition in Ritual

One way to build scriptural power in a shared fashion, in a community, is to use specific words over and over. In one church I served, we used the same words each Sunday morning to open our worship service:

> This day is a gift, a gift of love, a gift from God, a gift from life itself. Come, let us worship together. This is the day we have been given, to live in, to love in, and in time to die in. Let us be grateful for the incredible gifts of life. Let us rejoice in the promise and possibilities of this day.

Though written by my colleague, Mark Christian, those words belonged to the whole church. They went far beyond worship. Some people used them in their own daily spiritual practice. More than once, parishioners quoted them to me as giving insight in a particular circumstance. One young boy told his mother, "I don't ever want you to die, but I know that this is the day we have been given, to live in, to love in, and in time to die in." What an astounding gift that the church has given him, to begin to understand mortality based on words that he hears ritually in church.

Words used frequently at ceremonial occasions such as memorial services, weddings, coming-of-age services, or new-member welcomes can have the same impact. By living with a text year after year, the meanings seep into our souls at a more profound level, and our understandings deepen. They become associated with the lives of people we love and shape our worldview. They also provide a shared perspective with others who gather in our congregation. Too often, Unitarian Universalists jump at innovation and novelty, seeking originality in their practices, without regard for how meaning grows in people's hearts and minds. Helping to determine our congregation's core ideals and reflecting them regularly by using the same words in our ritual, in our meetings—wherever we gather together—can provide texts that become scriptural for an entire congregation.

Scripture and Music

Though Unitarian Universalist tradition tends to be heavy on words, music is one place where we, like most religious traditions, effectively combine the verbal with the artistic. Throughout history, music has drawn from scriptural texts for words. Music has helped people in many different cultures around the world memorize stories and doctrine. Adding dimensions to the words through rhythm, melody, and harmony enriches our connection with a text and cements it in our memory. *Singing the Living Tradition* includes hymns drawn from Psalms (lots of these!), Confucius, Genesis, Hindu prayers, Sutra Nopata, Isaiah, Micah, and various traditional texts, including a Texcoco Nahuatl poem. The reading at the end of this chapter will consider a biblical passage that has become a common Unitarian Universalist hymn.

Most people don't notice the source of the words of a hymn or anthem (the central musical piece sung by a choir). Investigating sources can enrich listening to or singing the words. Hymns generally note a source, and an order of service may give the source of an anthem's words. If a song captures one's imagination, it's worth digging a little deeper and finding the words in their original context, a task made much easier with Google!

Weaving Scriptural Reference

Exemplary preachers and speakers recognize and engage with striking images and stories. Scripture, being laden with such elements, provides a wealth of resources. Abraham Lincoln drew on the image of "the house divided." Mahatma Gandhi spoke of "renouncing fruits of action." Emerson wove images from Eastern and Western scriptures into his essays and poetry. Bits of scripture can appear in opening and closing words, in prayers and meditations, or in sermons and stories. A scripture quotation could be printed in an order of service or projected onto a screen for contemplation prior to the service or during a time of meditation.

Should scriptural sources, then, be identified as texts are woven in? Traditionally, many preachers—including Unitarian Universalists—have quoted scripture without naming its source, particularly in earlier centuries when biblical references were more likely to be recognized. Today, we might be able to drop the latest Internet meme without attribution, but few people will be familiar with scripture unless we have worked to introduce it. At the same time, you may not want to distract listeners with long citations. Preachers and worship leaders must take care to balance different needs and come up with the best answer for any quotation within a specific context.

For example, the scriptural source of an anthem or introit can be acknowledged in an order of service. If scripture is used as a reading, context can certainly be introduced; then, in subsequent references to the text, little detail is needed. When echoing short scriptural phrases in an artistic way, however, particularly in meditation or prayer, citations can be distracting. Overall, if we use a particular scriptural passage often enough that the congregation develops a greater familiarity with it, we may no longer need frequent citations. Part of explaining the context of scripture takes place in worship, but this explanation also involves a larger commitment to religious education and all the other areas of congregational life.

A Reading from Isaiah

The spirit of the Lord GOD is upon me,
because the LORD has anointed me;
he has sent me to bring good news to the
    oppressed, to bind up the brokenhearted,
to proclaim liberty to the captives, and release
    to the prisoners; to proclaim the year of the
    LORD's favor,
and the day of vengeance of our God;
to comfort all who mourn; to provide for those
    who mourn in Zion—to give them a garland
    instead of ashes,
the oil of gladness instead of mourning,
the mantle of praise instead of a faint spirit.
They will be called oaks of righteousness, the
    planting of the LORD, to display his glory.
    They shall build up the ancient ruins,
they shall raise up the former devastations;
they shall repair the ruined cities, the
    devastations of many generations.

> Isaiah 61:1–4, The Hebrew Bible,
> New Revised Standard Version

MANY UNITARIAN UNIVERSALISTS will recognize these words from the prophet Isaiah because they have sung them many times in Carolyn McDade's popular hymn, "We'll Build a Land" in *Singing the Living Tradition*. Though the words are ordered differently in the two, the images are identical: binding up the broken, freeing captives, the oil of gladness dissolving mourning, bringing good tidings, garlands replacing ashes, rebuilding of ancient cities, raising up devastations of old, mantles of praises coming from spirits that were faint, and the people as oaks of righteousness.

The same scripture passage makes an appearance among the readings in the back of the hymnal, in these edited words:

> The spirit of God has sent me to bring good news to the oppressed, to bind up the broken-hearted, to proclaim liberty to the captives and release to the prisoners, to comfort all who mourn, to give them a garland instead of ashes, the oil of gladness instead of mourning, the mantle of praise instead of a faint spirit. They shall build up the ancient ruins, they shall raise up the former devastations, the devastations of many generations. You shall be named ministers of our God.

These images, even as they are shaped and revised in our hymnal, are outside the culture of a lot of contemporary Americans who don't smear their faces with ashes when they mourn or apply oils to match their moods. Garlands and mantles are hardly part of their daily lives. Yet, the expressions are engrained in our culture, and singing them speaks to us, particularly with a lively waltz rhythm and compelling tune.

The poetry captures us, and so does the meaning. The speaker in the original passage is likely the third Isaiah, a prophet who lived during and after the Babylonian exile, when the many Israelites, including leaders and the wealthy, had been removed and then returned to their land of Israel. Imagine people who have been broken and held captive returning home to a land that has been devastated by conquest. The tasks that must be done would seem overwhelming, impossible. And yet, the leadership must encourage everyone to embrace the challenge before them.

While the post-exilic prophet is describing and encouraging the process under way among his people, rebuilding their homeland, Christians have traditionally seen the book of Isaiah as messianic, predicting the coming of a chosen one, a savior, who will bring these good things to the people. In fact, the gospel of Luke tells of Jesus reading these very words from the scroll in the synagogue and declaring himself to be the person spoken of.

As Unitarian Universalists sing "We'll build a land," we are identifying with the prophet Isaiah and with the teacher Jesus as we proclaim their words about transforming the world. This is consistent with the Unitarian Universalist christology and our commitment to making a better world. We tend to identify with the human Jesus and try to live the life he gave as example. We want to join in making this world better. The metaphors may be old, but the spirit dwells in them as it dwells in us.

Native American Unitarian Universalists have critiqued the hymn because of the imperialism inherent in the historical conquest of the American continents by Europeans. Whose land has been taken in order to build the ideal described? This raises the complex issue of how scripture has been used to support acquisition of land and oppression of people, in the Americas and in Asia, Africa, the Middle East, and the Pacific—and not only by Christians. The search for a holy land by one people has often displaced other people whose roots were deep in a particular place. We have to consider what we mean to create and how we mean to create it. Nations and "lands" are not created from nothing. Can we bring a wider vision of inclusion to a hymn whose content may raise legitimate trepidation for some of us?

Lifting voices in song brings us together as a community while we make a commitment. One of the differences between the book of Isaiah and the lyrics of the song is the pronouns. Isaiah uses singular pronouns, even though the community of Israel was not individualistic. McDade changes the pronouns to plural; the song we sing is about "us," not "me," and about "we," not "I." We don't take on these formidable tasks alone, but together, in the plural. This is further symbolized by the raising of voices in song—or in the responsive reading of the passage—in a communal setting, a worship function of com-mitment and unity. The question remains: Who does "we" include? That's critical in determining whether we can build a new land. Is this code for taking a land from others? Can "we" include everyone? Can this be a real vision of building Beloved Community, or is it fatally compromised by white colonialism?

What's more, not everyone who sings believes in the "Lord God" of Isaiah; in fact, few, if any in a Unitarian Universalist congregation are likely to espouse a traditional view of the

Hebrew God. The presence of the Lord in the lyrics has been reduced to "anointed by God" in the chorus, words interpreted metaphorically by many Unitarian Universalists. The responsive reading does begin with the spirit of God (not "Lord," though) and skips forward to end with a tiny piece of the sixth verse of the chapter: "you shall be named ministers of our God."

In the song lyrics, the remainder of the chapter, verses five through eleven, are completely omitted. These verses tell about the judgment that the Lord will bring against those who have oppressed the Hebrews and how the foreigners will come to be their servants. The righteous, then, are identified with the Hebrews and their God, while the oppressors will get what they deserve. This division exemplifies the struggles that have long existed in the Middle East, where each side rightfully can claim that the other side has stolen from them. Hoping for a day when foreigners become one's servants perpetuates rather than heals the wounds of oppression. No wonder we omit these verses. Knowing they are there provides a useful warning.

This latter part of the chapter casts a shadow over the beautiful image of renewing a promised land. It demonstrates the problems so often inherent in scriptural texts, and the ways people writing in a particular place and time pass on their own biases and judgments. Certainly, a conquered people newly returned to a ruined home will carry bitterness; it shows in the text. We cannot pass judgment on those who have experienced something we have not. However, we can be on guard as to how we read and interpret the words.

McDade has gone in a different direction from the text and found another way to end her song, turning to the prophet

Amos for images of justice and peace as flowing water. The words once again sound familiar, as they play in our heads in the voice of Martin Luther King Jr.: "Let justice roll down like waters and righteousness like a mighty stream." Amos is often translated as including *judgment*, rather than *justice*. So, each of the readers—McDade and King—who have reinterpreted the scripture and brought it to life for us has recast it a bit for their own purposes.

Though some folks want to hold onto one firm, eternal meaning and may object to such revisions, when scripture is alive to us, that's exactly what we do—take its images and words and make them our own. With the hymn "We'll Build a Land," and with the responsive reading, we Unitarian Universalists have found resonance, though not complete congruence or agreement with the ancient Hebrews. Like them, we find value in building a world, in envisioning a Beloved Community and striving to make it real. What better sentiment to express in worship with voices raised together, while remembering the cautionary tales?

CHAPTER ELEVEN

Beyond Study and Worship

The Master said, "If a man [sic] who knows the
three hundred *Odes* by heart fails when given
administrative responsibilities and proves incapable
of exercising his own initiative when sent to
foreign states, then what use are the *Odes* to him,
however many he may have learned?"

Analects of Confucius 13:5,
translated by D.C. Lau

WHEN WE THINK of scripture, we often relegate it to the two
particular areas of congregational life we have already discussed:
religious education and worship. What if scripture could have
a larger presence? How might it enhance congregational life?
Already, you might see scripture crop up in a variety of settings
in your congregation. Small groups such as covenant groups
use scripture readings as openings and closings. Boards or other
decision-making groups may call on scripture to set a particular tone. Scripture can provide words of comfort when
someone is ill or struggling. Often, in Unitarian Universalist
settings, these uses of scripture are accidental and incidental.

How could we use scripture more intentionally to lead us to new and powerful understandings of our own lives?

The greatest effect of scripture comes when we see ourselves in the stories and revelations. If we can suspend our disbelief and enter into passages, then when we need them, they come to us almost automatically to guide our journey.

For example, when Martin Luther King Jr. spoke of seeing the Promised Land and added, "I may not get there with you," he drew on his followers' multifaceted and nuanced understanding of the Exodus journey. The images from the end of Deuteronomy in particular, in which Moses blesses the Hebrews, came to people's minds. Moses led his people through the wilderness for forty years but died in sight of their new home. When King said, "I've been to the mountaintop," followers who knew their Bible imagined Moses at Mount Sinai, glimpsing God, and then imagined him blessing his successor, Joshua, and lying down to die. The images resonated with them and deepened the experience and meaning of King's words. The drama played out more richly because they shared textual context.

Such echoes can be hard to duplicate among Unitarian Universalists because we have few texts that hold more meaning and guidance for us than others. There are so many texts that we could immerse ourselves in that we often choose "none of the above." And yet, we do develop *individual* preferences. Many Unitarian Universalists will tell you particular texts or quotations that help guide their lives. They pop up on Facebook or in printed notecards, are hung on bulletin boards or engraved on bookplates. You may find an excerpt from Thich

Nhat Hanh or Ecclesiastes, from the Bhagavad-Gita or Denise Levertov. The words may not all be formally recognized as religious scripture, but these iconic passages hold scriptural power for the people who prize them.

Scripture in Pastoral Care

When someone is very ill, hearing words from beloved texts offers comfort. When someone is grief-stricken, remembering the words they heard while their loved one was still alive keeps their presence alive to them. Even people with Alzheimer's disease perk up when they join in words buried deeply in their consciousness, like Psalm 23 or a familiar hymn. This is scripture doing its work. This reminds us of the need to be familiar with the text beforehand, so that the literature can do its job when it is most needed.

I have heard Unitarian Universalists bemoan the fact that they have nothing like that to rely on when they need it. This argues for using certain texts earlier and more regularly, in preparation for a time when they can be shared together in a pastoral moment or alone in seeking comfort.

When I was a young minister, I received a late-night phone call from a parishioner. Her father had just died. I was exhausted and had nothing to offer, but it was clear I needed to go be with her and her family. As I parked my car at the curb and walked toward her sister's house, I prayed that I would find some way to be helpful. I went in and hugged family members and offered condolences, then accompanied my parishioner to the bedside where her dead father lay. I had no idea how to comfort her. Then, she said, "Would you sing 'Amazing Grace'?" I sang four verses from memory. The words and music did the ministry. A familiar, comforting set of words could offer more than any creative reassurances an exhausted minister could have come up with in the moment.

Unitarian Universalist minister Laurel Hallman, in her curriculum *Living by Heart*, recommends the spiritual practice of memorizing poetry that has personal meaning. The idea is to have that poetry available as a resource in life. When words become part of the strata of someone's life, they have attained the status of scripture. A minister or someone else offering pastoral care may need to know what particular passages have meaning or power for an individual. A pastoral caregiver can ask what has brought comfort before. Reading or reciting meaningful texts, even if a person is unconscious, may provide healing and support that cannot be accounted for in a scientific way.

Themes in Congregational Life

There are older traditions of which we all should be aware and have as tools in our spiritual kit. An increasingly popular practice in our congregations is the selection of monthly themes and stories to use throughout the church, as a way of living more deeply into our stories. By using theme-based ministry, congregations integrate worship, religious education for children and adults, newsletter and online features, and small group ministry—as many programs as they can—to address similar concepts throughout the month. The entire congregation considers one theme.

Not all theme-based ministry includes connections with scripture or story. However, the inclusion of a story related to the theme intensifies the effect. Stories increase the memorability of what is taught, help us step into the experience, and ornament the ideas. This process allows the theme to blossom into more than a concept or abstraction. Stories make it real—stories that have persisted over generations by being stamped with the label of scripture are the best kind to use.

Some of the very best stories occur in multiple scriptures in different versions. Take, for example, the story of the blind men and the elephant. Many are familiar with this tale, which describes how one person felt the tail and thought the elephant was like a rope, how another felt the tusk and thought the elephant was like a spear, how another felt the body and thought the elephant was like a wall, how another felt the leg and thought the elephant was like a tree, and how another felt the trunk and thought the elephant was like a snake. The Buddha tells the story in Udana (68–69), a Pali Buddhist text of sayings of the Buddha. Jains take the story from Tattvarthaslokavatika of Vidyanandi (ninth century) and Syādvādamanjari of Ācārya Mallisena (thirteenth century). The Sufi poet Rumi includes it in his *Tales from Masnavi*, a book that is foundational to Sufism. The story's long pedigree and staying power argue for its inclusion as a scripture to delve into deeply.

If the story served as the congregational theme for a month, it would be told in worship at least once and form the basis of a sermon. Children in religious education might explore the way different senses tell different things about the world, as they taste, smell, touch, see, and hear. They might videotape "eyewitnesses" of a set-up event to compare what different people observe. Youth might consider the need to find a collective view of truth by looking at and perhaps drawing a complex centerpiece from different directions. They might talk about how different perspectives play out in their lives at school and in their families. Adults might explore the theme through discussions in covenant groups, or through viewing and talking about a movie like *Crash*, in which multiple stories and points of view are interwoven and collide, literally and figuratively. Ministers and religious educators could suggest activities for families to engage in around the theme and write reflection columns in their newsletter and blogs that expand on some aspect of the story. The whole congregation, then, would experience the tale together, adding shared meaning, vocabulary, and ideas.

The next month, the congregation might explore the creation story from Genesis, and the next, the Buddha's enlightenment. They might even tackle something that could be considered specifically Unitarian Universalist scripture, such as a passage from Thoreau's *Walden*, or the "five smooth stones" outlined in James Luther Adams's essay, "Guiding Principles for a Free Faith." Suggested themes and stories are included in the Appendix at the end of this book.

As the use of themes has increased in Unitarian Universalist congregations, various resources have developed. At least two subscription services exist for themed materials: the Touchstones Project (mdduua.org/download/touchstones/

Touchstones-Subscriptions.pdf) and Soul Matters (soulmatters sharingcircle.com). In addition, see *Sparks of Wonder: Theme-Based Ministry for the Whole Congregation* by Becky Brooks and Erika Hewitt, published by Skinner House Books. The Unitarian Universalist Association provides extensive information on theme-based ministry on its website as well, at uua.org/re/themes.

Sharing these experiences congregation-wide deepens our connection to one another, gives us a common religious language, and opens us to a shared sense of the holy.

Secondary Uses of Scripture

Even when we're using scripture in a smaller way, it can help to make meaning by setting our lives in a context. When we use opening and closing words for a group or meeting, selection deserves a careful process. Instead of picking out favorite words or something that seems to fit the subject of the meeting in a shallow way, a leader might consider what story we're living together at this time in our church life and what scripture might reflect on that.

Maybe the community has recently had a shocking loss. Even if grief is not the purpose of the meeting, hearing a psalm or a lament from Gilgamesh might soothe participants. This is an enlargement of the pastoral care we spoke of earlier. Much as a text may be helpful to an individual, so it may aid a community in getting through its struggle.

In a time of ministerial transition, it could be helpful to hear a story of another community's leadership transition. When starting a march or social justice project, hearing something from the Hebrew prophets or the ethical texts of Buddhism could inspire participants. The idea is to give a more universal context to our own experience by bringing scripture to bear on what we're doing.

Building Traditions Around Scripture

Communion in the Christian church can be a ritual enactment of a story or a reminder of the story. Passover in the Jewish tradition does the same thing with a different story. Our congregations can engage with meaningful stories and live into them in similar ways.

In one church I served, each Sunday between Christmas and New Year's, the "Stone Soup" story was shared. A variety of different versions had been used, but they always included the core story of one or more wanderers who enter a suspicious village and cook stone soup, using a stone, of course, but also whatever ingredients they can talk the villagers into sharing. The sharing results in a celebration like none before, so it becomes a story of building community.

More important than sharing the story, though, was the enactment. Before the story, everyone brought their contribution to the kitchen: chopped carrots, diced onions, cans of beans, pasta, cut-up meat. During the service, volunteers made both meat-based and vegetarian soups. Afterward, everyone shared lunch together. The story of building community became an incarnation of building community.

Many Unitarian Universalist congregations tell the story of Norbert Fabián Čapek and use his flower blessing as part of a service of Flower Communion. The blessing becomes incarnated scripture. These rituals become part of the lifeblood of a community.

The Value of Shared Understandings

Scripture can have tremendous power in our personal lives. We can relate to stories, poetry, proverbs, and even doctrines through study and spiritual practice.

The ultimate test for scripture, though, is its use in a community of people. When we develop shared understandings, we grow together as a people and create something amazing, a support system and home for ourselves and also for those to come. What's more, we connect with the past so we form a span of community that extends in all temporal directions. When we read or recite together, we become one in ways that transcend ordinary experience.

I have witnessed the power scripture can hold, particularly in more theologically conservative churches. I have seen scripture work that way from time to time in Unitarian Universalism; I'd like to see that spiritual power become more integrated into our journeys together.

Let us embrace scripture, then, study it, question it, read it together and individually, and make it ours.

In closing, I will share about how a particular passage has shaped my own ministry.

A Reading from the Tao Te Ching

The highest type of ruler is one of whose
    existence the people are barely aware.
Next comes one whom they love and praise.
Next comes one whom they fear.
Next comes one whom they despise and defy.

When you are lacking in faith,
Others will be unfaithful to you.

The Sage is self-effacing and scanty of words.
When his [sic] task is accomplished and things
    have been completed,
All the people say, "We ourselves have
    achieved it!"

        Tao Te Ching 17, attributed to Lao Tzu,
        translated by John C. H. Wu

THE TEXT STRUCK ME from the first time I saw it. I recognized myself as the leader who liked to be loved and praised. Because I pursued that, even when I was unaware that I was doing so, I often found myself as one who received love and praise. I came to realize, though, the limitations inherent in that. My own needs could hold back the community, if I stayed focused on my own ego. I could be manipulated through compliments. I could overtax myself, investing more in doing for others than they themselves were investing. I could lose track of what mattered.

Then, one day, a man explained something to me in the very words I had given him, though he did not seem to realize where the words had come from. The concepts had become his so thoroughly that he did not remember where he had acquired them. On that occasion, I did not remind him where he had learned his ideas, but treasured my own knowledge that I had made a difference. This incident symbolized for me the leader "of whose existence the people are barely aware."

How could I become the leader who didn't need the praise and love of people, but only needed to make a difference? How could I be the leader who the people barely notice, because they are convinced that they have done it themselves? And how to do so in a way that truly honors the transformation of the people I strive to lead, plus transform myself through my interactions with them? These longings stayed in front of me with this reading.

I have read many different translations of these words, whose origins are hard to pin down. Attributed to Lao Tzu, the Tao Te Ching emerged centuries before the Common Era and has been translated into English more times than any book except the Bible. Maybe that is because "The *Tao* that can be told is not the eternal *Tao*," as the first line of it proclaims. Scholars disagree about whether Lao Tzu was even a real person, or a mythic figure based on a conglomerate of community elders. Over time, interpreters have speculated about his role. Taoists saw him as a counter to the structure of Confucian code that tried to establish order in chaotic times. Whoever wrote the words, however they came to be, the writer understood something essential about the use of power.

The classical Taoist approach didn't establish a set of rules, instead encouraging a harmony with the universe that espoused the practice of *wu-wei*, usually translated as "non-action," though it does not mean literally doing nothing. Rather, *wu-wei* means acting without ego investment, effortlessly in harmony with the movement of the universe. I learned something of it in my practice of Tai Chi, in which each repositioning of arm or leg must be accomplished with as little effort as possible. Tai Chi, whose origins are late, has adopted Taoist interpretations. This kind of effortless effort creates a setting where people take little notice of their leader, so they become barely aware of her existence.

The text is not arguing for a leader who is ineffective, who literally does nothing, but for a leader whose movement is so subtle and so attuned with the people that they can do more than the leader could possibly do alone, or that they would do without the leader. Leadership becomes the facilitation of collaboration. A radical form of humility is required, along with a trust—a faith—in the people's ability.

These words of the Tao Te Ching have rung out for me and anchored me through much of my ministry. For my installation service at First Unitarian Church of Oklahoma City, Music Director and Composer-in-Residence Beverly McLarry set them to music, and the choir sang them. When I have found myself too concerned with getting credit, I have turned back to the words. When I have offered too many words, I have reminded myself of the sage's scanty words. I have prayed over these words, reflected on them, and held myself up to their standard. This scripture has made a difference in my life and, I hope, in the lives of those I have served.

My wish for you, dear reader, is that you, too, might find scriptures that you can hinge your life on, and that your congregation can find texts to live out into the future.

Suggested Scriptures and Stories for Theme-Based Ministry

Identifying core stories to accompany theme-based ministry increases the accessibility and memorability of the themes. Stories for theme-based ministry need not stick to scriptural sources. Integrating stories from Unitarian Universalist history, from other historical sources, from contemporary sources, and even from science will enrich and deepen a program. However, the topic of this book is scripture, so here are some suggested stories from (broadly conceived) scriptural sources, narratives that beg for familiarity. Each is listed with potential themes:

Abrahamic Scriptures

Creation, Genesis 1:1–2:3. Themes: creativity, order, God, sabbath

Moses in the Bulrushes, Exodus 1–2:10. Themes: family (adoption), oppression

The Exodus from Egypt, Exodus 5–15. Themes: freedom, oppression, liberation

David and Goliath, I Samuel 17. Themes: bullying, courage, overcoming odds

Ruth and Naomi, Ruth. Themes: family, loyalty, covenant

The Good Samaritan, Luke 10:25–37. Themes: compassion, otherness, hospitality

The Prodigal Son, Luke 15:11–32. Themes: reconciliation, forgiveness

The Night Journey of Muhammad (Isra and Mi'raj), Sahih Muslim, Book 1, Number 309. Themes: heaven, mysticism, human struggle to worship

Asian Sources

The Blind Men and the Elephant, Udana 68–69, available at cs.princeton.edu/~rywang/berkeley/258/parable.html. Themes: perspective, difference, pluralism

The Tao Is Like Water, Tao Te Ching 8. Themes: flexibility, letting go, the elements

The Parable of the Carpenter and the Oak Tree (The Worthless Tree), Chuang Tzu Section 4. Themes: purpose, judgment

The Seed and the Salt, Chandogya Upanishad, Sixth Prapathaka (Adyaya), Twelfth and Thirteenth Khandas, available at hinduwebsite.com/sacredscripts/hinduism/upanishads/chandogya.asp or in Fahs's *From Long Ago and Many Lands*. Themes: essence, God, mystery

Buddha's Enlightenment, The Buddha-karita of Asvaghosha. Themes: suffering, enlightenment, balance (the Middle Way)

Mustard Seed Medicine, original, Therigatha VI.1 and VI.2, available in Fahs's *From Long Ago and Many Lands.* Themes: death, grief

Amaterasu, Kojiki Kamatsumaki, First Volume. Themes: sun, anger, forgiveness

Other Scriptures

Utnapishtim's Story of the Great Flood, Gilgamesh Tablet 11. Themes: immortality, natural disaster

Persephone and Demeter, Greek myth. Themes: grief, loss, seasons

Stone Soup, European folk tale, available at pitt.edu/~dash/ type1548.html. Themes: community, generosity, hospitality

Sky Woman and Turtle Island, various oral Iroquois versions, Haudenosaunee, available at historymuseum.ca/cmc/ exhibitions/aborig/fp/fpz2f22e.shtml. Themes: creation, elements, home

Acknowledgments

W‌HEN I BEGAN this endeavor, I could not have imagined how many people would end up touching this book. It sounds trite to say it could not have been written by myself alone without the support of innumerable individuals. However, when speaking about scripture and religious practice, I have to say that the interdependence that exists must be acknowledged as spiritual practice. I have gratitude for everyone who has made this book possible, though I cannot possibly list every name.

First, several people reviewed the text for accuracy concerning the various traditions included in the book. I am especially grateful to Vishal Agarwal, Bruce Kafer, Sam Trumbore, Wayne Arnason, and Jaye Starr. Also, I appreciate the following reviewers: Ranwa Hammamy, Michael Motia, Glenn Willis, Louis Komjathy, Ben Williams, Ari Gordon, Emily

Mace, Orlanda Brugnola (deceased), Erik Walker Wikstrom, Kelly Weisman Asprooth-Jackson, Marti Keller, Kat Liu, and Jonipher Kwong. Their input and that of other reviewers has drastically bettered the book. Of course, any errors that remain are mine alone.

A number of my Harvard Divinity School professors deserve mention because, though that was more than twenty years ago, they influenced the way I read texts. William Graham, Annemarie Schimmel, and Inés Talamantez opened my eyes to the breadth of what religious texts can include and mean. Jon Levenson shaped my understanding of Judaism and Christianity as sibling religions. Ted Hiebert and Bernadette Brooten introduced me to biblical scholarship. Richard Valentasis, Krister Stendahl, and Ruth Roper helped me learn the relation between scripture and worship.

Of course, my learning did not stop with seminary. Special acknowledgement goes to my teachers of spiritual direction at HeartPaths: Bob Gardenhire, Curt Gruel, and Kay Morgan for helping me take scripture personally through immersion.

During the time I wrote this book, I served two different congregations, First Unitarian Church of Oklahoma City, and the Unitarian Universalist Fellowship of Manhattan, Kansas, whose love and support allowed me to engage deeply with this material. Janice Martin, the lay leader with whom I co-taught adult religious education for many years in Oklahoma City, including classes in world religions, helped to inspire the writing of this book. Among the classes we taught was one based on the *Eternally Compelling* online curriculum, written by Cindi Brown and Dr. Cynthia Stewart. Though my contact with them has been virtual, the inspiration provided by their work led directly to this book. Also helping inspire my work with scripture, along with a broad definition of what qualifies, has been the Reverend Doctor Laurel Hallman and her curriculum, *Living by Heart*.

I would be remiss if I neglected my thanks to Skinner House and, particularly, Mary Benard, who guided me with care through the process of creation. Mary has been patient and persistent. Her commitment to accuracy and quality led us both down unexpected paths. She went above and beyond in shaping what you read here; it would not have been the same without her.

Finally, my companion and life partner Jane Powell told me she doesn't need to be acknowledged. But, without her, I could not be on the path I'm on.

Resources

Agarwal, Vishal, Sacred Hindu Scriptures and Languages—an Introduction, unpublished draft provided by the author.

Armstrong, Karen, *The Bible: A Biography*. New York: Grove Press, 2007.

Armstrong, Karen, *Islam: A Short History*. New York: Modern Library, Random House, 2002.

Arnason, Wayne, and Kathleen Rolenz, *Worship That Works: Theory and Practice for Unitarian Universalists*. Boston: Skinner House, 2008.

Buehrens, John A., *Understanding the Bible: An Introduction for Skeptics, Seekers, and Religious Liberals*. Boston: Beacon Press, 2004.

Confucius, *The Analects (Lun yü)*, trans. with introduction by D. C. Lau. New York: Penguin Books, 1979.

Conze, Edward, *Buddhist Scriptures*. New York: Penguin Books, 1959.

Coogan, Michael D., *Eastern Religions: Hinduism, Buddhism, Taoism, Confucianism, Shinto*. New York: Oxford University Press, 2005.

Cragg, Kenneth, *Readings in the Qur'an*. London: Harper Collins, 1988.

Davis, Kenneth C., *Don't Know Much About the Bible: Everything You Need to Know About the Good Book but Never Learned*. New York: Eagle Brook, 1998.

Easwaran, Eknath, *The Dhammapada: A Classic of Indian Spirituality*, 2nd ed. Tomales, CA: Nilgiri Press, 2007.

Easwaran, Eknath, *Passage Meditation: Bringing the Deep Wisdom of the Heart into Daily Life*, 3rd ed. Tomales, CA: Nilgiri Press, 2008.

Ehrman, Bart D., *Misquoting Jesus: The Story Behind Who Changed the Bible and Why*. San Francisco: Harper Collins, 2005.

Gandhi, Mahatma, *The Bhagavad Gita According to Gandhi*. Berkeley, CA: North Atlantic Books, 2009.

Gottwald, Norman K., *The Hebrew Bible: A Socio-Literary Introduction*. Philadelphia: Fortress Press, 1985.

Gutiérrez, Gustavo, *A Theology of Liberation: History, Politics, and Salvation*, 15th anniversary ed., trans. Caridad Inda and John Eagleson. Maryknoll, NY: Orbis, 1988.

Hallman, Laurel, *Living by Heart: A Guide to Daily Devotional Practice*. Video and workbook.

Hanson, Rick, with Richard Mendius, *Buddha's Brain: The Practical Neuroscience of Happiness, Love & Wisdom*. Oakland, CA: New Harbinger Publications, 2009.

Hopkins, Dwight N., *Introducing Black Theology of Liberation*. Maryknoll, NY: Orbis, 1999.

Hunt, Mary E., and Diann L. Neu, eds. *New Feminist Christianity: Many Voices, Many Views*. Woodstock, VT: Skylight Paths Publishing, 2010.

Levine, Amy-Jill, and Marc Zvi Brettler, *The Jewish Annotated New Testament: New Revised Standard Version Bible Translation*. New York: Oxford University Press, 2011.

McAuliffe, Jane Dammen, ed., *The Cambridge Companion to the Qur'an*. New York: Cambridge University Press, 2006.

Neihardt, John (as told to), *Black Elk Speaks: Being the Life Story of a Holy Man of the Oglala Sioux*, premier edition, annotated by Raymond J. DeMallie. Albany, NY: Excelsior Editions, State University of New York Press, 2008.

Nhat Hanh, Thich, *Being Peace*. Berkeley, CA: Parallax Press, 1987.

Nylan, Michael, *The Five "Confucian" Classics*. New Haven: Yale University Press, 2001.

Osborne, Richard, and Borin Van Loon, *Introducing Eastern Philosophy*. New York: Totem Books, 1996.

Pine, Red, trans. and commentary, *The Heart Sutra: The Womb of the Buddhas*. Washington, D.C.: Shoemaker & Hoard, 2004.

Rahman, Imam Jamal, *Spiritual Gems of Islam: Insights and Practices from the Qur'an, Hadith, Rumi & Muslim Teaching Stories to Enlighten the Heart & Mind*. Woodstock, VT: Skylight Paths, 2013.

Rosen, Steven J., *Essential Hinduism*. Westport, CT: Praeger, 2006.

Schimmel, Annemarie, *Islam: An Introduction*. Albany, NY: State University of New York, 1992.

Schüssler Fiorenza, Elisabeth, *In Memory of Her: A Feminist Theological Reconstruction of Christian Origins*, 10th ed. New York: Crossroads Publishing, 1994.

Smart, Ninian, and Richard D. Hecht, ed., *Sacred Texts of the World: A Universal Anthology*. New York: Crossroad, 1984.

Smith, Wilfred Cantwell, *What Is Scripture? A Comparative Approach*. Minneapolis: Fortress Press, 1993.

Tsu, Lao, *Tao Te Ching*, Gia-Fu Feng and Jane English, trans., with Toinette Lippe. New York: Vintage Books, 2011.

Wing, R. L., *The Illustrated I Ching*. New York: Dolphin Books/ Doubleday & Co, 1982.

Notes

1. E.H. Rick, Jarow, "Emerson's Gita: Krishna and the Tradition of Conscience," rickjarow.com/articles/Emerson's%20Gita.pdf.
2. Ninian Smart and Richard D. Hecht, eds., *Sacred Texts of the World: A Universal Anthology* (New York: Crossroad Publishing, 1982), xiv–xv.
3. Smart and Hecht, xv.
4. Wilfred Cantwell Smith, *What Is Scripture? A Comparative Approach* (Minneapolis: Fortress Press, 1993), 18.
5. Smith, 212.
6. Norman K. Gottwald, *The Hebrew Bible: A Socio-Literary Introduction* (Philadephia: Fortress Press, 1985), 95.
7. Flavius Josephus, *The Works of Flavius Josephus*, William Whiston, trans. (Philadelphia: Lippincott, 1856), 515.
8. Edward Conze, *Buddhist Scriptures* (New York: Penguin Books, 1959), 11.
9. The most complete collection of these is probably at sacred-texts.com/index.htm.
10. "Native American Literature—selected bibliography," compiled by K. L. MacKay, faculty.weber.edu/kmackay/native_american_literature.htm.

11. Baruch Spinoza, *Theological-Political Treatise* chap. 12, G III.159/S (Cambridge, MA: Hackett, 2001), 145–6.

12. Winthrop S. Hudson and John Corrigan, *Religion in America* (Upper Saddle River, NJ: Prentice Hall, 1999), 259.

13. Swami Tyagananda, "Reflections on Hindu Studies vis-à-vis Hindu Practice," religion.barnard.edu/overview-hindu-studies.

14. James H. Cone, *Risks of Faith: The Emergence of a Black Theology of Liberation, 1968–1998* (Boston: Beacon Press, 1999), xiv.

15. James H. Cone, *A Black Theology of Liberation* (Maryknoll, NY: Orbis Books, 2010), 63–64.

16. huffingtonpost.com/j-mase-iii/josephine-reconciling-my-queer-faith_b_4014580.html.

17. Francesca Gino and Michael I. Norton, "Why Rituals Work," *Scientific American*, May 14, 2013, scientificamerican.com/article/why-rituals-work.

18. Aleister Crowley, *Magick, Book 4* (York Beach, ME: Samuel Weiser, Inc., 1994), 134.

19. Taittirīya Upaniṣhad 1.8, in Moore Gerety and Finnian McKean, *This Whole World Is OM: Song, Soteriology, and the Emergence of the Sacred Syllable*, Harvard University dissertation, dash.harvard.edu/handle/1/17467527.

20. "Two Monks Roll Up the Blinds: Zen and Rituals," by James Ishmael Ford, Roshi, July 2, 2001, boundlesswayzen.org/two-monks-roll-up-the-blinds.

21. Guigo II, *The Ladder of Four Rungs*, umilta.net/ladder.html.

22. This explanation comes primarily from R. Lawrence Kushner, who explains it in various Internet postings, including in an interview with Krista Tippett on her radio show "On Being": onbeing.org/program/lawrence-kushner-kabbalah-and-the-inner-life-of-god/6309.

23. Footnotes from the original text have been omitted.

24. *Midrash Rabbah*, "Foreword," by R. Dr. I. Epstein, archive.org/stream/RabbaGenesis/midrashrabbahgen027557mbp#page/n23/mode/2up, p. xviii.

25. *Anguished English*, Laurel Book published by Dell, a division of Random House, 1987, p. 137.

26. Amy-Jill Levine and Marc Zvi Brettler, eds., *The Jewish Annotated New Testament* (New York: Oxford Universitiy Press, 2011), 562.

27. Joseph Priestley, *A general view of the arguments for the unity of God; and against the divinity and pre-existence of Christ: from Reason, from the Scriptures, and from History* (Birmingham, England: Pearson and Rollason, 1788), babel.hathitrust.org/cgi/pt?id=njp.32101076400959;view=1up;seq=17.

28. Hosea Ballou, "A Letter to the Reader," *A Treatise on Atonement*, as published online by Dan Harper, danielharper.org/treatise.htm#toc.

29. Quillen Shinn, "Affirmations of Universalism," in *A Documentary History of Unitarian Universalism: Volume Two, from 1900 to the Present*, Dan McKanan, ed. (Boston: Skinner House, 2017), 8.

30. David E. Bumbaugh, "Is There a Humanist Vocabulary of Reverence?" in *A Language of Reverence*, Dean Grodzins, ed. (Chicago: Meadville Lombard Press, 2004), 21.

31. Laurel Hallman, "Images for Our Lives," in *A Language of Reverence*, 29.

32. T'ai-Shang Kan-Ying P'ien, *Treatise of the Exalted One on Response and Retribution*, Paul Carus, ed., Teitaro Suzuki and Paul Carus, trans. (CreateSpace, 2012).

33. Diana Eck, *A New Religious America: How a "Christian Country" Has Become the World's Most Religiously Diverse Nation* (San Francisco: HarperSan Francisco, 1997), 47.

34. Sophia Lyon Fahs, "For So the Children Come" in *Worshipping Together with Questioning Minds* (Boston: Beacon Press, 1965), 270.

35. Donald Carson, *Exegetical Fallacies*, fallacyfiles.org/quotcont.html.

36. Mahatma Gandhi, *The Bhagavad Gita According to Gandhi*, John Strohmeier, ed. (Berkeley, CA: North Atlantic Books, 2009), xxiv.

37. Marjorie Bowens-Wheatley, "Cornrows, Kwanzaa and Confusion: The Dilemma of Cultural Racism and Misappropriation," uua.org/multiculturalism/introduction/misappropriation/37852.shtml.

38. David Chapman, "Problems with Scripture," *Vividness* (blog), June 24, 2011, vividness.live/2011/06/24/problems-with-scripture.

39. Addison Hodges Hart, *The Ox-Herder and the Good Shepherd: Finding Christ on the Buddha's Path* (Grand Rapids, MI: Eerdmans Publishing Co., 2013), 56.

40. John G. Neihardt, *Black Elk Speaks, Being the Life Story of a Holy Man of the Oglala Sioux* (Lincoln: University of Nebraska Press, 1979), 38–39.

41. Neihardt, xi.

42. See: sites.google.com/site/colorsofthefourdirections/lakota. Neihardt notes that blue, as well as black, can represent the West.

43. Acharya Buddharakkhita, "Preface" to his translation of the Dhammapada, accesstoinsight.org/tipitaka/kn/dhp/dhp.intro.budd.html.

44. Wayne Arnason and Kathleen Rolenz, *Worship That Works: Theory and Practice for Unitarian Universalists* (Boston: Skinner House, 2008), 87–88.